BOOM
TOWN
NEWSPAPERS

Booming Last Chance Gulch in Helena, Montana, in 1865. The round-the-clock activity there prompted founding of rival newspapers—the *Montana Post* and *Helena Herald*. (Montana Historical Society, Helena.)

BOOM TOWN NEWSPAPERS

Journalism on the Rocky Mountain Mining Frontier, 1859-1881

David Fridtjof Halaas

FOREWORD BY RALPH LOONEY

UNIVERSITY OF NEW MEXICO PRESS : ALBUQUERQUE

Library of Congress Cataloging in Publication Data

Halaas, David Fridtjof.
  Boom town newspapers.

  Bibliography: p.
  Includes index.
  1. American newspapers—Rocky Mountains region—
History—19th century. I.   Title.
PN 4894. H34   071'.8   81–12932
ISBN 0–8263–0588–1   AACR2

Partial funding for the composition of
this book was provided by the Mellon
Foundation through a grant to the
American Association of University Presses.

DEDICATED TO
Marjorie Anne Gotchey Halaas

Contents

Illustrations

Acknowledgments

My profound appreciation to Dr. Eugene T. Halaas and Sylvia Halaas, who offered suggestions as only parents can. Their knowledge and understanding made this book possible.

"A tip of the hat and best bow" also to Col. (Ret.) Robert E. Gotchey and Albarose Gotchey; Rick Manzanares; Judy Schlueter; Clay Schulz; Dr. Marvin Jaffe; William L. Whitney, Jr.; Don and JoAnn Selchert; Dr. Charles Kutzleb; Dr. George P. Nicovich; and Robert A. Myre.

And to Fr. Michael Kavanagh, Pastor of St. James Church, Denver, and John F. Casey, both of whom were a combination of printer's devil and devil's advocate, my heartfelt thanks for their friendship.

Finally, for their wisdom and unfailing assistance, my deepest gratitude to Dr. Robert G. Athearn, my mentor at the University of Colorado, Boulder, who first suggested the topic to me, and who instilled in his graduate student an appreciation for the richness of the history of our Rocky Mountain west; Richard H. Shay, President of The Fairmount Cemetery Association, whose sense of history and writing was of invaluable help throughout the writing of this book; Caroline Bancroft, author of some thirty books on Colorado history, who gave so generously of her time to improve the manuscript; and Marjorie Anne Gotchey Halaas, my wife, for whom this book is dedicated.

Foreword

You can find thousands of books telling the story of America's western frontier, but precious few to report on the intrepid journalists who brought communication and news to a rough and untamed land. Strangely, the editors and printers have been neglected, in spite of their importance in the opening of the West.

Newspapers are vital to society, a linchpin of democracy and a most necessary component of civilization. They provide much more than just a report of the day's news and the goings-on at City Hall and the County Courthouse. They provide food for the intellect through a free exchange of ideas and opinion. They stimulate business and commerce by providing advertising space. They thwart tyranny by permitting an outlet for criticism of government. They are an essential ingredient of civilization and were a necessary element in the taming of the West.

David Fridtjof Halaas breaks new historical ground with his story of some of those often rambunctious newspapers and the men who created them on the Rocky Mountain mining frontier.

It is fascinating reading.

The subjects of Halaas' book were rare individuals who endured all kinds of hardship to produce newspapers under the most primitive and difficult circumstances. These were men who had to be able to handle every kind of job from reporter to editor to ad salesman to typesetter to pressman and even delivery and work seemingly endless hours to accomplish it.

The obstacles were enormous.

It was difficult enough to transport a heavy press and fonts of lead type by wagon over long miles of primitive trails against often hostile elements.

Once at the destination there was the problem of finding shelter to set up shop. That alone was a major task, since boom camps were little more than tent and shack towns often clinging to the walls of rocky canyons and thronged with crowds of men and animals. Streets were either flint-hard ruts choked with dust or hub-deep mudholes, depending on the weather. Rents, like prices of all kinds, were sky high.

In the case of William N. Byers, founder of Denver's *Rocky Mountain News,* the best quarters he could find was the attic over Uncle Dick Wooton's saloon and store. The light of one small window had to be supplemented with candles as Byers and a couple of printers frantically assembled the first edition in a race to beat a rival editor who had hit town a few days earlier. When a snowstrom struck and the roof began to leak like a sieve, Byers had to rig a tent over the press to prevent the printed pages from being ruined.

Such experiences were only the beginning of travail for a boom town editor.

There was also the matter of trying to sell advertising, solicit subscriptions, find enough news to fill the columns of the paper, pay for supplies and rent and so on ad infinitum, not to speak of dealing with offended readers who as often as not sought satisfaction from editors at the point of a six-shooter.

But in spite of the headaches editors persisted. They brought newspapers to such unlikely places as Buckskin Joe, Tubac, Tombstone, Mountain City and others. Some of the towns are long forgotten. Sometimes the papers failed. Sometimes it was the ore that petered out instead of the editor and the town died. Sometimes the papers endured.

I am fortunate to edit one of the survivors. The *Rocky Mountain News* in Denver, born in that boom camp saloon attic on Cherry Creek in 1859, is one of the great success stories of journalism. Today it circulates more newspapers daily than any newspaper in the Rocky Mountain West.

Author Halaas has a great understanding of journalism and what makes journalists tick. His research into the boom camp era has been painstaking and extensive. He has dug deeply into the files of boom camp newspapers to discover stories never told before.

The result is the chronicle of a dynamic period of journalism and a formidable number of determined men.

I'm sure you will find the story as fascinating as I did.

RALPH LOONEY
Denver, Colorado
August 1981

Preface

On July 8, 1859, just outside the low-lying adobe walls of Tubac, New Mexico Territory, two men, armed with Burnside rifles, conferred with their seconds. The details of the duel had been worked out earlier. Both Mr. Cross, the challenged party, and Mr. Mowry would have the opportunity of four shots, the affair to conclude only when Mr. Mowry declared himself satisfied, or if one of the principals was unable to continue.

A large crowd looked on, its size reflecting the fact that Tubac was no longer an insigificant wayside stop on Cooke's Wagon Road leading west to the California goldfields. Now, Tubac itself was something of a mining camp. The discovery of gold and silver in the nearby Santa Rita Mountains had brought with it an onrush of miners, swelling the population of the former Spanish *presidio* to more than eight hundred.

It was this relatively sudden populating of the isolated southwestern regions of New Mexico that lay behind the present difficulty between Mr. Cross and Mr. Mowry.

With vast stretches of hostile deserts and barren mountains separating the newcomers from the seat of government in Santa Fe, a movement began to create a new territory out of New Mexico. Already, the proposed territory had a name—*Arizona*—although its boundaries were still a subject of spirited debate.

Sylvester Mowry stood in the forefront of the Arizona movement. A graduate of West Point, Lieutenant Mowry served at various southern New Mexico outposts, including Mesilla, Tubac, Tucson, and Ft. Yuma. By 1858, after two years at Ft. Yuma, Mowry was convinced that only through separate territorial organization could the resources of southwestern New Mexico properly be developed. Accordingly, he resigned his commission in the army to work full-time for the creation of Arizona. His army experience, along with his charismatic personality and darkly handsome features, gained him considerable following. Twice, self-constituted territorial conventions elected him as Delegate to Congress. And twice, Congress refused to recognize the man from Arizona.

Undaunted, Mowry made the rounds, speaking to influential congressmen, senators, even to President Buchanan himself. By the early winter of 1858, Mowry could take some pride in his efforts. Not only was he making headway with senators such as Stephen A. Douglas of Illinois, chairman of the Committee on Territories, but even President Buchanan was impressed by the potential of Arizona. In his 1858 message to Congress, Buchanan spoke glowingly of the resources of the proposed territory and placed its population at 10,000, a figure given him by Mowry. Territorial organization seemed at hand.

In Cincinnati, Ohio, Edward E. Cross read the President's message with more than passing interest. A former editor of papers in New Hampshire and Ohio, Cross was a seasoned journalist and a hardened realist. He had heard the wild stories of the Arizona and Sonora mines, even had made a modest investment in the St. Louis and Arizona Mining Company. Still, he was not convinced. Not even the assurances of his close friends, Thomas and William Wrightson, officials of the Sonora Exploring and Mining Company headquartered in Tubac, completely satisfied him. He had to see for himself—and his chance came almost immediately. Several eastern newspapers asked him to act as their traveling correspondent and report regularly on the activities around Tubac and the Sonora mines. Cross readily agreed, and in company with William Wrightson, set off for Arizona.

When Cross arrived in Tubac, he encountered the usual trappings of a boom camp—miners in their odd and colorful garb; the predominance of drinking and gambling emporiums along the narrow, twisted roadways; the ne'er-do-wells and camp followers; the lawlessness and ever-present danger of sudden and unprovoked violence.

Cross, no stranger to the frontier, expected this. What surprised and disturbed him was the absence of feverish mining activity. The dry gulches surrounding Tubac showed no evidence of placer diggings, a prime requirement for a boom camp; and although signs of silver abounded, extracting the metal, he saw, would be an expensive, time-consuming process. For those who came for quick riches, Tubac was a bust, a cruel humbug. Cross, however, recognized the potential of the area. Well-financed mining companies had made Tubac their headquarters, and Congress was seriously considering southern New Mexico as a possible route of the transcontinental railroad. He knew, too, that future growth was dependent on steady immigration, not on false and exaggerated tales of a new Eldorado in the desert.

As a journalist, Cross understood the power of the printed word. Armed with his pen, he was determined to put a stop to the wildly speculative stories circulating in the East. It was this resolve that thrust him into the heart of the Arizona movement and his confrontation with Sylvester Mowry.

His opening salvo was a stunning one. Using the pen name of "Gila," Cross scribbled a letter, dated Tubac, January 30, 1859, and posted it to the St. Louis *Missouri Republican*. From here the *Washington States* (D.C.) picked up the story, printing it on February 26, under the eye-catching, bold-lettered heading: "Important from Arizona/THE HUMBUG EXPLODED!/the Gila Gold Mines a Failure, etc." Asserting that an enormous amount of falsehood had been published concerning Arizona, particularly of its resources and population, Cross disputed the President's population estimate of 10,000, calling it absurd. He also scoffed at the alleged wide plurality of votes cast for Sylvester Mowry electing him as Arizona's Delegate to Congress. Such a plurality, he said, "meant that *everybody* voted—men, women, children, Indians, and Greasers."

Twenty-five hundred miles away from Tubac, Mowry read the letter with growing anger. Not only did it reflect on his character as a gentleman, but it also threatened to ruin all his lobbying efforts in Washington on behalf of the Arizona movement. His reply, published in the *Washington States* on March 1, 1859, was a strongly worded defense of his population estimates and his assessment of the resources of Arizona. He concluded by warning "Gila": "I . . . have proved it by more evidence than . . . would be sufficient to hang twenty such fellows as the writer of this anonymous letter if he was on trial—a fate . . . which will be apt to overtake him when his letter gets back to Arizona. . . ."

More than a month passed before Mowry's letter reached Tubac; in the meantime, Cross had become editor of the Tubac *Weekly Arizonian*. Working out of a small, crowded adobe office with a Washington hand press, Cross used the columns of the *Arizonian* as a forum for his views, weekly sending his ragged four-page sheet to major newspapers in the East. To him, the Arizona movement was nothing more than an invention of power-hungry politicians. Rather than seek territorial organization, something Cross thought impossible, given the tensions between North and South, southwestern New Mexico should work for the establishment of a separate judicial district. This course would bring much needed troops to protect the roads against Indian harassment, as well as legally-constituted courts and law officials, and all this could be accomplished now within the present framework of New Mexico Territory.

To answer Mowry, Cross wrote directly to the *Washington States*, his letter appearing in that paper on May 24. He went straight to the point. He allowed that he had been "a careful reader of Mr. Mowry's voluminous (and, as I now find, *fabulous*) productions regarding this country, and supposed them correct. I found, however, that many of his assertions were not true, and that all were exaggerated." By circulating these "productions," Mowry, he said, was "absolutely injuring the Territory, and deluding people into a long and dangerous journey. . . ." As to the "hanging question," Cross saw no cause for alarm: "By the opinions every day expressed hereabouts who know [Mowry's] course, I apprehend that he is eminently more deserving and more in danger of lynch-law than myself."

The battle was joined. When Mowry read the letter he immediately left Washington for Arizona, reaching Tucson on June 30. Here he wrote his final reply, sending a copy to Cross in Tubac. This time he accused Cross and his "employer" in the Sonora Exploring and Mining Company of deliberately retarding the growth of Arizona for their own selfish reasons. Tired of further argument he issued his challenge: "The fact that I raised [Cross] to the level of a gentleman, by demanding of him personal satisfaction for the scurrilous language he has used toward me, prevent my showing him in his true light. . . ."

Now, on this hot July day, the battle of words was over, the distance reduced to forty paces. A strong cross wind kicked up clouds of dust, impairing vision and making further discussion useless. The seconds backed off, and at the command, a succession of shots rang out. Through the haze, onlookers thought the duel was over, that the allotted four shots had been exchanged. But again the seconds conferred, and word quickly spread that on Mowry's final fire, his rifle failed to discharge. All concerned agreed that Mowry was entitled to another shot. Cross stood impassively, his arms folded in front of him, waiting. Mowry aimed, then suddenly raised his gun and fired harmlessly in the air. Striding over to the surprised editor, Mowry declared himself satisfied and the two men clasped hands.[1]

The Cross-Mowry affair, an outgrowth of a boomlet to the southwestern desert regions of New Mexico, was a portent of what would come in later mining excitements on the Rocky Mountain mining frontier, from the Pike's Peak hysteria in the spring of 1859, to the Tombstone rush of the early 1880s. It is an indication of the seriousness with which camp newspapers and their editors were regarded, not only by the mining population, but also by eastern power brokers and capitalists, and prospective immigrants.

This study examines those newspapers founded in newly established boom camps along the Rocky Mountain front between 1859 and 1881. However, the present states of Utah and Idaho are excluded: Utah, because its papers were essentially religious and usually controlled by the Morman Church; and Idaho, because its mining journals tended to look westward and were associated more closely with the papers of Nevada, California, and the Pacific Northwest. Further, those newspapers identified with the Colorado silver rush of the late 1870s are outside the scope of this work. By the late seventies, Colorado had achieved statehood and the region was well-served by numerous railroads. Indeed, many of the Colorado silver camps were linked almost immediately by rail and telegraph with the outside world. This is reflected in the style and character of the silver camp journals and separates them from the camp papers of the early 1860s.

DAVID FRIDTJOF HALAAS
Aurora, Colorado
Spring 1981

The Rocky Mountain Mining Frontier

1

Peculiar Sheets
in a Peculiar
Setting

The rush to California in 1849 persuaded even the skeptical that the Far West was veined with gold. Easterners thrilled to stories, endlessly retold in hometown newspapers, of solitary miners striking it rich overnight and of rivers of gold still to be discovered. Romanticized, too, were the mining camps that sprang from the gulches and hillsides of that distant land. Tales about the wild and abandoned exuberance of camp life appealed to some Americans who were rooted by custom and circumstance to lives little changed from those of their forefathers. And many who remained behind wistfully cast their eyes westward and wished that they themselves had risked all and braved the long, arduous trek to the goldfields. But by the mid-fifties most realized that the time for quick and easy wealth had passeed them by, that they would have to wait for other discoveries and other diggings.

Their wait was not long. In the spring of 1859 Ohio and Missouri river towns emptied as tens of thousands of gold-crazed fortune hunters made their way to the junction of the South Platte River and Cherry Creek in a land known as the Pike's Peak Country. Yet the "Pike's Peak or Bust" excitement nearly died aborning. When the Fifty-niners pulled into the twin camps of Denver City and Auraria they met with heart-sickening disappointment. Instead of rivers of gold they found deserted diggings and a tent and log city crowded with saloons and hard-eyed gamblers. Shouting "Humbug!" many angrily wheeled their wagons around and headed back to the States. But the "Gobackers" left too soon. In June, Horace Greeley, the eccentric but highly acclaimed editor of the *New York Tribune,* penned a stirring message to the nation. After personally inspecting America's newest goldfield, Greeley pronounced it nearly equal to the California mines and assured all that gold could be found in the mountains just west of Denver City. His word was taken as gospel and the rush to the Central Rockies resumed.[1]

The Pike's Peak hysteria set in motion a general mineral exploration of the Rocky Mountain West. For the next three decades gold discoveries from New Mexico and Arizona to Colorado, Wyoming, and Montana sent thousands of eager prospectors into regions once thought fit only for Indians and venturesome fur trappers. "Cities"— instant communities boasting populations of thousands— made their appearance throughout the period and gave the mining West its style and character.

Although the camps came into existence at varying times and places, at their inception they were essentially alike. That is, Tombstone, Arizona, in the eighties differed only in degree from Central City, Colorado, or Virginia City, Montana, in the early sixties.[2] Isolated both by time and distance from settled regions, the camps shared similar birth pangs and initial days of unrest and feverish activity. Many were short-lived; but some quickly began to display apparent signs of permanency. Wood- and brick-constructed buildings, churches, schools and reading rooms were welcomed by townspeople as evidence that the new community had a future full of promise and prosperity.

Perhaps the most sought after improvement and one that excited the attention of all camp residents was the establishment of a local newspaper. A lively town paper was an ideal way of booming the camp and its surroundings, of attracting capitalists, laborers and settlers, of demonstrating to the world that life in the mining West was safe and civilized. The paper also helped to relieve the camp dweller's considerable literary thirst. As one Fifty-niner explained: "You who are surrounded by literature of all kinds cannot imagine with what eagerness I read all items, editorials, letters from the seat of war, lists of accidents, marriages and deaths, advertisements, etc. . . ."[3] When impassable roads and hostile Indians disrupted mail service the local newssheet often provided the only available reading material and helped many a miner pass idle hours and lonely nights. Thus, camp papers satisfied westerners' promotional demands as well as their deep-seated desire for a dependable source of news.

Editors, then, were quick to see the wisdom of Horace Greeley's advice, "Go West Young Man." Realizing the golden journalistic opportunities inherent in mining communities, men of print rushed to newly discovered diggings with an eagerness and intensity almost equal to that of the goldseekers. And like the goldseekers they were driven by the same hope—to arrive on the scene in time to stake out the choice claims.

The dramatic stampede of editors and printers to Cherry Creek in the spring of Fifty-nine was typical of what was to occur in other boom camps throughout the history of the Rocky Mountain mining frontier. Following a hectic and mud-splattering journey from Omaha, William N. Byers, a sometime surveyor and successful town promoter, arrived in the camps of Denver City and Auraria in mid-April expecting to be the first equipped journalist in the mining district. But he quickly found out that one Jack Merrick, a journeyman printer from Leavenworth, Kansas, had arrived several days earlier with press and type ready to publish his own paper. Ever resourceful, Byers had taken the precaution of printing the front and back covers of his four-page sheet before leaving Omaha, and, after negotiating for office space with Richens "Uncle Dick" Wootton, the owner of the "twin cities' " only two-floor wood building, he set about his own preparations. On April 22, three days after Byers' arrival, a whiskey-excited crowd "vibrated" between the competing print offices, watching latest developments and placing bets on the outcome of the "Battle of the Newspapers." Finally, at ten o'clock in the evening, Byers hurriedly distributed copies of his *Rocky Mountain News* to the awaiting populace. Jack Merrick's *Cherry Creek Pioneer* appeared but twenty minutes later, prompting a "self-constituted newspaper committee" to declare Byers the victor. The following morning a disappointed Merrick sold his press and type to his rival and set off for the mountains to pick gold instead of type.[4]

If Byers entertained the hope that by his victory over Merrick he had earned the corner on Denver's reading market, he soon was disappointed. Would-be journalists of every description were only too ready to spill printer's ink in the Pike's Peak Country. Shortly after the Byers-Merrick race, a visiting eastern correspondent commented on the host of newspapermen in Denver and warned that "printers, engravers on wood, stone and metals and Daguerreotypists, will find themselves compelled to work at something else or starve. Editors . . . are already plentifully supplied."[5] For the most part, his warning was ignored. Journalists continued their rush to Colorado and soon papers appeared in such remote places as Buckskin Joe, Canon City, Mountain City, and Golden.[6]

Later and in other locales, similar excitements gave birth to similar camp newspapers. Virginia City and Helena, Montana; South Pass City, Wyoming; Elizabethtown and Silver City, New Mexico; Tubac, Tucson, Tombstone and Prescott, Arizona—these were but a few of the camps that could boast of local newssheets shortly after their foundings.[7]

Rough and tumble boom camps, however, provided a unique and forbidding setting for journalistic efforts. Inhabitants of mining communities contrasted sharply with those encountered in established urban centers or country villages and hamlets. Thomas Dimsdale, a camp editor in Virginia City, Montana during its heyday, observed:

There can be scarcely conceived a greater or more apparent difference than exists between the staid and sedate inhabitants of rural districts, and the motley group of miners, professional men, and merchants, thickly interspersed with sharpers, refugees, and a full selection from the dangerous classes that swagger, armed to the teeth, through the diggings and infest the roads leading to the newly discovered gulches, where lies the object of their worship—gold.[8]

To gain the support of such a diverse gathering of people was a challenge facing every mining editor. Not that camp dwellers were illiterate or indifferent to events occuring outside the camp; far from it. The cry, "Mail's in!" invariably was greeted by long lines outside the post office and the unfortunate miner who failed to receive a letter or package from home was deeply disappointed. "Any delay in the arrival of mail," recalled one Colorado pioneer, "was wearing—how terribly so, none can know but those who have felt it."[9] Even so, for such a restless, floating population to lend its financial support to a local newssheet was a chancy proposition. Residents would have to be convinced that a camp paper would materially advance their interests.

The isolation of the camps also bode ill for western editors. Frequent delays in the arrival of the express and mails seriously handicapped editors who promised to keep readers abreast with the latest regional and national news. In an early issue, the Virginia City *Montana Post* happily announced that the mail had finally arrived, but noted at the same time that the news it contained was more than two months old.[10] The irregularity of mail service forced newsmen to keep a constant vigil for other sources of information. Wandering travelers often provided the only contact with the outside world, although the news they carried was often fraught with gossip and wild rumor. Without dependable channels of communication, western men of print would be sorely pressed to find a ready supply of newsworthy items.

Camp journalism was further belabored by crowded, primitive working conditions. Living space—hotel rooms, cabins, and tents—was at a premium and editors were forced to work wherever room was available. Many a boom camp newspaper was issued out of leaky attics, dark cellars, "dingy back rooms," "miserable cabins," and adobe holes-in-the-wall. Into these one room *sanctum sanctorums*, as editors invariably called their quarters, was crowded a vast array of equipment—presses, type cases, woodcuts, paper supplies—and some served double duty as sleeping quarters for editors and their staffs. On a visit to Denver, the noted British traveler, Charles Wentworth Dilke, was surprised and not a little impressed by the harsh conditions confronting mountain editors. "Till I had seen the editors rooms in Denver," he admitted, "I had no conception of the point to which discomfort could be carried. For all these hardships, payment is small and slow."[11]

Equipment, too, reflected the primitive environment. Most camp papers were issued on bulky Washington hand presses. These throwbacks to an earlier era of American journalism were capable of producing, with much patience and strenuous work, about two hundred copies an hour. First, the paper had to be moistened by sponge, the type inked and then the heavy lever tugged to bring contact between paper and type, once for each side. When this very physical process was completed, the sheets were hung to dry, hand-folded, and finally creased with a flat instrument, usually a whale bone. Only after all this was the paper ready for the public's critical eye.[12]

Under the best of conditions no editor's life was easy. A roaring boom camp with its frenzied pace only made matters worse. Time and again frontier editors attacked readers who expected their mountain sheet to be equal to that of large eastern papers. "Considering that one or two men do that in the mountains which a half score or half hundred do in the Hub or on Manhattan," wrote one overburdened Montana scribe, "you may have patience and forgiveness, if your appetite is unsatiated. We will stop this, right here; nobody but a country editor will ever appreciate it."[13] Further, the overabundance of printers in the camps, at least initially, did not guarantee editors a permanent, reliable staff of assistants. On the contrary, most editors found themselves, at one time or another, doubling as typesetters, pressmen, news carriers and, as one laconically put it, "God only knows what else."[14]

Even if blessed with steady and competent help, their days were long and taxing. Besides reading letters and scanning exchanges, they spent the daylight hours making the rounds of the camp keeping abreast with latest developments, visiting nearby diggings to watch and evaluate the progress of the mines, answering the endless questions of new arrivals and supervising the printing of job work and other sundry assignments. After a short break for dinner, they secluded themselves in what they fondly called their *sanctum sanctorum,* or den, and scribbled reports on what they had seen during the day. If not occupied with meeting deadlines, there were letters to write, records to keep, visitors to entertain, and always bills to pay. Embittered by the long hours and low pay, many vowed never again to take pen in hand to edit a newspaper. In a parting shot at thankless subscribers, one weary Tucson editor had this to say to his fellow townsmen:

We have not been in the business long enough to become misanthropic but we begin to feel it coming on, and we throw down the quill entertaining the belief that more is expected of a country editor for less money than from any other person on earth. And if in the course of human events he grows sordid, morose, cross, cussed and mean, it is not his fault but the fault of those who receive the benefits of his toil and then abuse him for it. So kind readers, adieu, and may the good Lord have mercy on your souls.[15]

The rough and ragged appearance of camp papers further reflected the conditions under which they were published. The typical product was a weekly four-page sheet containing anywhere from three to seven columns a page. National and foreign news, clipped from eastern exchanges, usually dominated the cover, along with what were announced as the "latest telegraphic" communications. Editorials, mining intelligence (or news), and discourses on town and regional issues met the reader on the second page. These items usually were original, although "gleanings" picked up from nearby papers appeared as well. The following page was devoted to local and personal news. Here, readers could peruse the latest town gossip, enjoy "puffs" of enterprising merchants and honored camp arrivals, study weather reports of outlying districts and puzzle over the editor's thoughtful worries about any topic he deemed important. Finally, the last page contained miscellaneous articles, essays, poems—anything necessary to fill an empty column.[16]

Dominating the camp press was the large space given up to advertising. It was not uncommon for nearly half the paper's total columns to be filled with personal cards of shopkeepers and sales announcements of every conceivable description. Advertisements, of course, were a major source of revenue for all newspapers—but on the frontier they were valued for other reasons as well. The insertion of numerous business and personal notices could be taken as evidence of the community's wide-awake, enterprising spirit. Therefore, lest uninformed or distant readers make the false assumption that the camp and its paper were tottering on the brink of bust, editors sometimes found it expedient to fill their columns with "dead ads" and unsolicited business cards, a practice neighboring and equally devious rivals were quick to expose. "In our sheet," boasted one, "you will find no time tables on distant and to us unimportant railroads and stage routes, none of the spurious dead ads so often used in sluggish communities to fill up space in the local papers. On the contrary we are obliged by the rush of advertising to enlarge our paper in order to give even our usual amount of reading matter."[17]

Small as these papers were, editors battled valiantly to insure journalistic professionalism and that town dwellers could read their paper with pride. But the hostile frontier environment was a constant spoiler. Road closures, careless freight drivers,[18] thefts along the highways, and Indian wars made regular shipment of vital supplies usually only a vague hope for the future. One hardened Colorado newspaper veteran recalled that he acquired considerable expertise in "printing on wrapping paper, druggists' paper—we cleaned out what little druggists' paper there was—tissue paper, in fact any kind of paper we could get, and we missed several issues in the summer of '59 because there was nothing to print on."[19] Another inventive editor reported that for weeks he had gone to press on dark wrapping paper and now his sheet was "in a dubiously colored suit which even the fond fancy of an Editor cannot recognize as a 'pink' of perfection."[20] Complaining that a year's supply of paper was laying in wait at Salt Lake City because spring rains had washed out roads preventing shipment, the intrepid editor vowed to present his journal "in the best form possible, either on paper, shingles or . . . the caudal appendage of an inside blouse. We will never say die while there's a shot in the locker."[21]

Typographical and grammatical errors also marred the appearance of camp papers. Despite every effort to correct proofs, errors slipped by with maddening frequency. One weary editor readily admitted to his errors, but offered the explanation that "we hardly pretend to see at all after four o'clock in the morning. Glasses do us no good. The result is, errors of the most common character are as likely to escape us as those which are seldom seen."[22]

Quick to temper, many editors were outraged when their errors were pointed out. One excused his grammatical inconsistencies by saying:

We do not claim absolute perfection in typography, orthography or even grammatical constructions. We are usually busily engaged from the time we get up in the morning . . . until after dark with our general business. We write our copy after supper and receive the proof sheets from the hands of our compositors at midnight. We are weary and often overlook errors, and even then when accurately marked, the compositor's eyes, which have been strained for hours in setting type by lamp light, fail to see the errors marked. Under such circumstances it is difficult to be absolutely accurate, or at all times to avoid gross blunders.[23]

Another editor testily responded to criticism by declaring: "We dislike verbal criticism because it is almost always contemptible, and therefore we have been silent in regard to the numerous grammatical . . . sins of our neighbor, although he has called attention . . . to every slip of the pen and typos that have appeared in our columns."[24] Noting that his accuser had committed innumerable "crudities, stupidities and gross violations of English grammar," he reproduced a few samples of the "scholastic errors" abounding in his neighbor's columns.[25]

The imperfect physical appearance and the typographical peculiarities of mountain papers belied their serious intent. Editors penned lengthy articles justifying the paper's existence and seized every opportunity to remind subscribers of the indispensable role a local newssheet played in the growth of the community. A local paper, they argued, was the most effective way to promote the camp and its resources, to induce immigration, and to gain the attention and financial support of important eastern capitalists. For most editors, booming the camp was the most obvious purpose for the newspaper. Frank Hall, a pioneer editor in Black Hawk and Central City, Colorado, summed up the purpose of his sheet this way:

Our circulation extends to almost every state in the Union, and to many parts of Europe. Those people are to be favorably impressed with the country and induced to emigrate hither, bring capital, science, labor and all the elements that are so essential in building up a new state. We want creative power in this grand work of ours, not unproductive consumption.[26]

Similarly, the *Mining Life* of Silver City, New Mexico, announced that it would be a "medium through which the world may learn of our whereabouts and resources. . . ."[27]

Out of necessity, the camp paper functioned as a kind of local chamber of commerce, for the future of the paper was dependent upon the survival and growth of the town. Without steady immigration both were doomed. Editors endlessly promoted the camp and its environs—the diggings were always the richest yet discovered, the soil the most fertile, the climate healthy, mild, and therapeutic, the merchants active and enterprising, and local "ladies" beautiful and attired according to the latest Paris fashions. During a visit to Prescott, Arizona, a correspondent for the *Sacramento Union* included in a dispatch a listing of the various business houses established in the camp and added a personal note that Prescott even possessed a "brass band and newspaper office—the two last, I presume, were established to 'blow' and 'puff' the other institutions; but I must do them the credit that, although somewhat windy, they are nevertheless meritorious institutions in their way."[28]

Camp papers, then, were careful to keep a watchful eye on the East and on prospective emigrants. Indeed, one editor freely admitted that much of the material in his columns was aimed not so much for the gratification of local townsfolk as for those living abroad.[29] As a public service for those who had made the decision to go West, editors published what they touted as reliable maps detailing the best routes of travel, offered advise on the equipment and provisions needed in the mining country and, of course, provided the latest news from the mines. In the first issue of Denver's *Rocky Mountain News*, prospective immigrants were warned that mining activity was hard, often futile work and urged all who were coming to bring their own set of tools and at least three months supply of provisions and clothing to tide them over in the event they were unable to find immediate or permanent employment.[30] Other regular news features described the camp and its surroundings along with editorials answering the many questions asked by distant readers.

The importance of eastern readers, however, did not deter western journalists from emphasizing issues and events of purely local import. Editors were aware that townsfolk sorely missed a home newspaper and promised to devote much time in their columns to personal and local items. In Deer Lodge, Montana, the editor of a weekly paper promised that he would "strictly attend" to local interests and work tirelessly in the people's behalf for needed camp improvements.[31] To insure that local news was fully covered most camp papers acquired the services of a local reporter who would make the rounds of the camp and report on every day events. Locals, as they were familiarly known, covered the construction of new buildings and homes, the arrival and departure of visitors, the culinary talents of town chefs and were always ready to write a friendly—or not so friendly—item for friends and acquaintances. Merchants were praised for the variety and quality of their goods, residents complimented for their diligence and enterprise, and rival neighboring sheets shown the errors of their ways. Nor were they beyond commenting on the activities of the saloon and dancehall crowds. Brawls and shootings were, in the main, faithfully reported, often accompanied by stern warnings that rowdy conduct would not be tolerated.

In reporting lawlessness, locals reflected the deep-seated belief held by their editors that newspapers had a duty to fight injustice, to elevate the moral tone of society, and to instill a sense of community and civic pride into the random gathering of people that together made up the camp's population. American journalistic tradition had long held that newspapers should be a positive, constructive force in the community; in the mining West, with its restless population and highly conspicuous criminal class, camp editors usually set about the dangerous task of at last tempering disruptive elements. As the editor of the *Arizona Daily Star* put it, a newspaper "promotes or retards material interests, elevates or degrades the standard of public morals, refines or debases the tastes, purifies or corrupts politics, and in every respect is an education of the people and a power for good or evil."[32] Saloonkeepers and dancehall proprietors were attacked in editorials when their establishments became the scene of frequent violent behavior. Individuals who consistently engaged in rowdy activity were told to mend their ways or move elsewhere. Road agents, horse thieves, and unscrupulous gamblers were given notice that although crime may have gone unchecked in the past, the time for acts of violence had passed and the camp stood ready to bring criminals to justice. Finally, when the legal organs of law and order were unable to combat effectively the lawless elements, editors did not hesitate to call for vigilante justice or the rule of "Judge Lynch."

At the same time that they attacked violence, editors reminded residents that they were participating in a great adventure—the settlement and civilizing of the West. Any activity that materially aided the town or contributed to its stability was the subject of much attention and editors were indefatigable in their efforts to encourage the establishment of permanent institutions. Residents were told to support schools, to attend church services, to observe the Sabbath, and to patronize local stores and businesses. Civic meetings were carefully attended and reported, theater performances reviewed, political meetings evaluated, and issues of western interest debated. If the camp needed a jailhouse, a post office, a firehouse, then town leaders were called upon to perform their civic duty and build them. And always they had a word of encouragement to those who suffered setbacks. During dull times, the camp press urged residents not to lose hope or despair—current difficulties, they counseled, were sure to pass and the diggings would yet prove their promise.

Still, as much as they wanted to inform, enlighten and entertain, it was not always possible for camp editors to fill their sheets with timely exposés or morale-uplifting news. Even the most imaginative were forced on occasion to admit that times were depressed and newsworthy stories scarce. "Scarce," lamented one editor, "We mean locals—anything startling, terrific or bloody. Our town is most excessively dull . . . no nothing except an abortive shooting escape [sic] and one suit for the collection of a whiskey bill."[33] Another complained:

Nothing exciting seems to move the inhabitants . . . the era of "big scares" and "stunning rumors" has been superceded by a state of morbid quietude extremely painful to the daily chronicler of current events, and one is almost tempted to turn Ranger or do something desperate to inqugerate [sic] a new state of things and startle the drowsy ear of deliberate unconcern."[34]

In an attempt to be interesting and lively, columns abounded with attempts at humor, with "gleanings," or items lifted from other papers that were several months old—even the ragged doggerels of local aspiring poets found their way into print.

Editors well understood that should they fail to provide a lively sheet, one that appealed to both home and distant readers, the future of their paper and perhaps even that of the town was seriously threat-

ened. No one expected the sheet to be alive with news when telegraph lines were down or when mail service was disrupted. Yet readers
did expect some items of local interest to appear regardless of conditions—a requirement many editors believed unreasonable. As one
said: "We have received several dig's in the rib about the dullness of
our paper, and how devoid of news it was. On this question we feel
like the boy did when the ass kicked him."[35]

News or no news, dull times or boom, camp editors made herculean
efforts to express themselves in a spirited, lively manner. This natural
predilection, combined with the seriousness of their mission and the
volatile atmosphere of the camp, often caused them to use language
that was highly personal, sometimes sensational, and even shrill.
So-called personal journalism, with its vituperative and abrasive style,
flourished in the camps, especially in those where several newspapers
struggled to gain the support of a limited number of subscribers.
Much of what was written was intended to be humorous; but editors,
like small boys slinging mud, were often carried away by the force of
their rhetoric and exchanged bitter, intemperate words with their
rivals that scarcely could bring credit upon themselves or favorably
impress distant readers.

For example, when Thomas Gibson of the *Colorado Weekly Republican* (Denver) heard about his across-town rival suffering a hu-
miliation at the hands of a woman he gleefully reported:

A VILLIAN HORSE-WHIPPED!! SERVED HIM RIGHT!!! Byers, the
editor of the *News*, was today HORSE-WHIPPED *in his own den*, by a lady
of this city, whom he had most grossly insulted by placing her name on a
burlesque election ticket. It is said that he bellowed and whined like a
whipped spaniel while undergoing the penalty of his meanness.[36]

This kind of villification and personal abuse was by no means restricted to rival editors. Delinquent subscribers, ungrateful readers,
political opponents, town loafers—all were subjected to editorial wrath.
But while personal journalism certainly enlivened an otherwise dull
sheet, most editors came to the realization that readers soon tired of
the practice. As William Byers, himself no stranger to journalistic
abuse, pointed out in 1866:

It is high time that western journals should take a higher tone and cease to
descend to the use of the vulgar and cant phrases that disgrace their columns. The publication of articles that verge upon the obscene simply be-

cause of their pot-house wit should be discontinued. Such things charm only the vulgar who, it is well known, are not the most profitable class of readers.[37]

The camp press was guilty of similar excesses when promoting the camp and the advantages of western life. In Prescott, the editor of the *Weekly Arizona Miner* acknowledged that "some time in the past, our zeal for progress and development may have caused us to tinge facts with roseate hues," but he hastened to add that the *Miner* never had "willfully" lied or misrepresented the resources of northern Arizona.[38] Editors shared the belief that people in the States were woefully misinformed about the extent and riches of western mines. Thus, while they were indignant when charged with giving credence to "false rumors"[39] or circulating deliberate fabrications, they were not above overstating the known facts. As one Black Hawk, Colorado, editor candidly admitted, "our papers do their best to exhibit the resources and wants of the country, frequently exaggerating them in order to make an impression."[40] What passed as the pleasantries of camp life, too, were presented in their most favorable light. "In violation of the rule of physics," wrote one editor, "something was manufactured out of nothing . . . when facts were lacking. Every maiden, who was married, blossomed by aid of cold type, into a lovely and accomplished bride. All stump speakers were metamorphosed [sic] by the same process into eloquent orators and profound statesmen. . . ."[41]

And so, out of isolated mountain valleys and gulches, with all their imperfections and crudities, whether in a fit of pink or on white, dark, or tissue paper, camp journals sent forth their messages to the world. That they could survive in such an environment or work under such primitive conditions was a source of wonder and amusement to many eastern readers. After scanning the contents of a newssheet published in the heart of the Rocky Mountains, one eastern editor made this puzzled observation: "The peculiar locality from which it is issued, and the peculiar circumstances under which the enterprise is inaugurated, makes it an object of peculiar interest."[42] And a correspondent of the *Missouri Republican*, after witnessing the establishment of a camp paper in Mountain City, Colorado, in the spring of 1859, was equally confounded:

The *Gold Reporter and Mountain City Herald* printing office strikes one as quite an anomaly, if considered in conjunction with the aboriginal appearance of the valley generally. It appears like a premature shoot-off, revealing energy of growth, but little vitality for lasting character. The proprietor of the concern, however, is determined to see the thing out. Whether he will be able to battle successfully with the immense volumes of snow and ice with which this valley is said to be visited during the winter, remains to be seen.[43]

The fate of all camp papers was dependent upon the fate of the camp itself. But even in the liveliest of camps, there was nothing inevitable about the survival of any sheet. Much depended on those who ventured into the mining West with their "shirttails full of type," eager to begin a new life in a new land.

2

"Shirttails Full of Type"

Not with pick and pan but with their "shirttails full of type,"[1] frontier men of print made their way to the Rocky Mountain mining camps determined to help shape the growth and development of the new land. Possessed of an abiding faith in the West, they set about their self-appointed role of promoting the camp and its neighborhood, of attracting immigration, capital, and labor. They did all they could to bring stability and permanency to their adopted community and the very nature of these activities thrust them into the forefront of camp life. In Last Chance Gulch, Montana, on the banks of Cherry Creek, Colorado, in the Moreno goldfields of New Mexico—wherever they chanced to settle and practice their profession, western editors assumed positions of community leadership and often were numbered among the camp's most influential residents.

Despite commitments to the community and its future, when circumstances dictated it, or when the diggings played out, editors were not hesitant to pull up stakes and seek new opportunities in other, more promising regions. Indeed, for many this search became a journalistic odyssey, an endless quest for the right camp with the right promise. One such wanderer was Thomas Gibson. A Britisher by birth,[2] Gibson entered into a newspaper partnership with William N. Byers and in the spring of 1859 was one of the founders of the *Rocky Mountain News* in Denver City. Within a few months, Gibson sold his interest in the paper and set off for Mountain City (later Central City) where he established his own sheet, the *Rocky Mountain Gold Reporter and Mountain City Herald.* Although he was well-received by Mountain City residents, he retired his infant paper in the fall of 1859 after only a few months of sporadic publication and allowed the Boston Town Company of nearby Golden City to hire his printing office to issue the *Western Mountaineer*. Shortly thereafter he returned to the States, purchased a newer, more elaborate printing outfit and on May 1, 1860 published Denver City's first daily newspaper, the *Daily Herald and Rocky Mountain Advertiser*. At the same time, Gibson issued the *Rocky Mountain Herald*, a weekly product he hoped would drive out his across-town rival and former partner, William Byers. Despite being locked in a heated and intensely personal press war with Byers, he managed to find time to slip out of the camp and travel to distant Canon City, where he founded the *Canon City Times*. 1861 found the irrepressible editor back in Mountain City, now called Central City, here to give birth to yet another paper, the *Mining Life*. Meanwhile, his battle with Byers was going badly and in an attempt to garner new support he changed the name of his weekly to the *Colorado Republican and Rocky Mountain Herald*, later shortening the title to the *Commonwealth and Republican*. Even after all this, his efforts were in vain. In January, 1864, after directly or indirectly founding six pioneer Colorado newspapers, Thomas Gibson sold his papers and left the Territory never to return as a journalist.[3]

Although Gibson's experience in frontier journalism was by no means uncommon, other western editors were more fortunate. The career of John H. Mills is representative of many camp editors who, after an uncertain beginning, eventually became successful journalists. A Civil War veteran accustomed to excitement and adventure, Mills found life in his native Ohio too quiet for his restless spirit and in the spring of 1866 he journeyed to the Yellowstone River Country to try his hand at mining. After losing his accumulated fortune by an ill-advised investment in a bogus hydraulic mining company, Mills settled in Virginia City, Montana, where he found employment as a bookkeeper. His long-range goal was to open his own wholesale leather store, but his skill with a pen brought him to the attention of the owners of the *Montana Post*. When the editor of that paper died, the proprietors asked Mills to assume temporarily the *Post's* editorial chair. Although without experience in journalism, Mills performed well as an editor. Accordingly, when the owners decided to move the paper from Virginia City to Helena, they asked Mills to stay on, this time on a permanent basis. In Helena, Mills faced a powerful competitor, the *Helena Herald*, edited by the famed Fisk brothers.[4] For two years Mills struggled to keep the *Post* alive, but finally, in July 1869, the challenge by the Fisks proved to be too great and he was forced to suspend operations. By this time, however, he had acquired a broad-based, loyal readership and with the financial backing of his many friends, he left Helena for Deer Lodge, Montana where he founded the *New North-West*. Here he continued his brisk rivalry with the Fisk brothers, only now with more success. For the next two decades James Mills, as owner and editor of the *New North-West,* was a powerful champion for Deer Lodge and a prominent figure in Montana politics.[5]

The careers of James Mills and Thomas Gibson are representative of those western journalists who possessed sufficient capital to purchase a complete printing office, who founded their own newspapers, and who then experienced ultimate success or failure. There were many others, however, who could not afford the high cost of establishing their own papers, who drifted from one camp paper to another, and who never quite failed or dramatically excelled in their profession. One such journeyman printer was Daniel G. Scouten who began his checkered career in 1867 when residents of Valmont, Colorado, requested him to edit the *Valmont Bulletin*. As editor of the *Bulletin*, Scouten soon ran into trouble with residents of nearby Boulder City who felt that the *Bulletin* abused their interests. As a result, a group of that camp's "finest," knowing Scouten's inordinate fondness for a "dram or two," invited the unsuspecting editor to a local saloon and while Scouten was thus distracted, his detractors loaded his press into a wagon and carted it off to Boulder. When Scouten learned of the action he "took the change like a philosopher, and promptly issued the first newspaper the town of Boulder ever had."[6] For the next year, he dutifully edited the *Boulder Valley News*, but not entirely to the camp's satisfaction. Scouten's proclivity for liquor was by this time well-known, and the paper's new owners began searching for a more reliable, disciplined editor. Finally, in 1869, Julius Wharton, formerly of the *Colorado Miner*, was brought down from Georgetown to manage the sheet and Scouten at last stepped aside.[7] His next journalistic effort came in Elibzabethtown, New Mexico, where he edited the *Moreno Lantern*. Again he met with disappointment. The Moreno goldfields were not proving their promise and Elizabethtown, after a brief boom, rapidly began to lose population. Scouten, therefore, found it impossible to gain the support of local merchants or to excite reader attention. In October of 1869, the Santa Fe *Daily New Mexican* reported that "the *Moreno Lantern* is dead. The editor went *scooting* out of Elizabethtown between two days followed by an enthusiastic constable who had the vain hope of overtaking and collecting a small board bill. . . . He has gone to hunt a more congenial clime and cheap democratic whiskey."[8] In April, 1870, Scouten was back in Boulder, again editing the *Boulder County News.* Still, the owners of the *News* did not have full confidence in their erstwhile editor. Whenever another could be found, they unceremoniously demoted Scouten to assistant editor, to local reporter—even to the pressroom. After three years of irregular work with the *News,* Scouten left Boulder for Longmont, Colorado, and accepted a position with the *Longmont Press.*[9] Then, like many other journeyman printers, he drifted away for a destination unknown.

Whether they found success or not, whether they roamed aimlessly or settled in one camp, western editors had much in common. In the first place, most were relatively young when they traveled to the goldfields to ply their trade. Of course, the mining West in general attracted young men who by nature were optimistic and adventuresome and who were strong enough to endure the hardships of the frontier. Camp editors were no different. For example, P.W. Dooner began his association with the *Arizonan* (Tucson) when he was twenty-eight;[10] Daniel Scouten was thirty when he started with the *Moreno Lantern;*[11] Edward A. Slack was twenty-seven when he was editor of the *South Pass News* (Wyoming);[12] and William N. Byers was twenty-eight when he founded the *Rocky Mountain News.*[13]

Not that all camp editors were young. Alfred Thomson, founder of the *Tri-Weekly Miners' Register* in Central City, Colorado, had years of editorial experience in the States before embarking on a career in the West. But he admitted in his first issue that on the frontier his advanced age would probably work against him. Unlike most introductory editorials, Thomson was pessimistic about his chances for success and warned readers that "this enterprise we have undertaken is, under the most favorable circumstances, an extremely hazardous one," and unless the citizens of Central City actively supported him "the experiment must prove a failure."[14] Nine months later, tired and his health broken, Thomson announced that he was leaving the paper and turning it over to younger, more ambitious men. In his farewell he acknowledged that "we doubt not our patrons will be very much obliged to us for retiring, when they see the improvement it has caused in the conduct of the *Register.*"[15] While it was not impossible for older men to edit mountain sheets, camp journalism favored young men who were physically able to withstand the rigors of the climate and the primitive conditions inherent in mining communities.

Most camp editors were also united by their lack of formal, academic schooling. Indeed, some had never worked on a newspaper, even as copyboy or "printer's devil." When Frank H. Woody wrote his "Salutatory" for the *Montana Pioneer* (Missoula), he begged the indulgence of his readers, informing them that this was his "maiden" attempt at journalism.[16] Similarly, David C. Collier was without experience when he began editing the *Tri-Weekly Miners' Register* in Central City, Colorado, although he did have a formal education. A graduate of Oberlin College, Collier studied law and was admitted to the bar in 1858. When rumors of gold reached Wyandotte, Kansas, where he had settled, he made his way to the Cherry Creek diggings and was one of the first lawyers to practice in Denver City. In 1862 he moved to Central City where he struck a close friendship with Alfred Thomson, editor of the *Tri-Weekly Miners' Register*. It was through his friendship with Thomson that Collier wrote occasional articles for the *Register*, and when Thomson decided to bow out, Collier assumed the editorial duties of the paper and eventually became one of its proprietors.[17]

John Wasson is perhaps more typical of those who lacked journalistic experience. Self-educated, Wasson had farmed in his native Ohio, tried his luck at mining in California, had taught school and then, upon arriving in Tucson, Arizona, in 1870, became the first editor of the *Arizona Citizen*. When he retired seven years later he wrote: "Although never desiring to enter journalism in Arizona, we have been satisfactorily paid for our labor. . . ."[18] It is noteworthy that Wasson sold out to John P. Clum, yet another frontier editor who was new to journalism.[19]

While a formal education was a rarity among frontier editors, most had experience as practical printers before beginning their western careers. A Montana editor observed that most of his associates had been "disciplined through experience, passing through all the gradations incident to the business, and were equipped with a breath of thought, versatility of ideas and expression, and fertility of resources only to be acquired through such a training."[20] Robert Tilney, editor of the *Boulder County News*, was of the opinion that a formal education was a liability to frontier editors. According to Tilney:

There are occasions which call for the highest skill in the expression of thought and the use of language, but those are comparatively rare. . . . Again, there are people who suppose that a man of learning and scholarship must be a competent editor. Not one in thousand of the scholars or savans

[sic] could keep a newspaper alive a single week. The contributions of these gentlemen are heavier ballast than any newspaper can afford to carry.[21]

More important than the ability to turn a good phrase or write a well-constructed essay was a thorough understanding of the inner workings of a printing establishment. Without the luxury of a reliable staff, frontier editors filled in as pressmen, compositors, and even newscarriers. Out of necessity, then, it was the rare editor who lacked prior training. Most had been associated with newspapers during their youth, often serving an apprenticeship on their home town papers. John L. Dailey, for example, had virtually no formal schooling but did occasionally attend a country school when not helping his father work the family's fertile Ohio farm. At seventeen, Dailey became an apprentice printer on a small "literary" paper, the *Laurel Wreath* in Fort Wayne, Indiana. When the paper folded, Dailey moved on to the *Fort Wayne Times* where he got a taste of the editorial room and the fine art of editing. After three years apprenticeship with the *Times*, he struck out on his own working as a printer for several newspapers in Des Moines and Omaha. It was in Omaha where he met the land speculator and town promoter, William N. Byers. When Byers left Omaha to establish a paper in the Pike's Peak Country, Dailey accompanied him, eager for the opportunity to become more than a mere printer or press foreman. In July of 1859, he bought an interest in the *Rocky Mountain News* and continued his relationship with the paper until his retirement in 1870. Dailey's experience as a practical printer proved to be of vital importance to the *News* and allowed Byers the freedom to be absent from the paper weeks, even months at a time. While Byers deserves the credit for establishing the *Rocky Mountain News* as one of the mining West's leading journals, it was Dailey, the practical printer, who was the steadying force, who saw to it that deadlines were met and who managed the paper's daily affairs.[22]

More than a practical printer's knowledge, however, was needed in the rough mining environment. Western journalists worked in densely populated camps where residents were crowded into a limited number of cabins, tents, boarding houses, and hotels. The newspaper office stood amid this congestion, and it was impossible for editors to isolate themselves from the general activity of the camp. To the camp's populace, editors were highly visible and easy to reach; when disgruntled readers wanted to have a "word or two" with them about a topic or a recent article, they had to be ready and able to defend their position and themselves. William Byers of Denver's *Rocky Mountain News* described this peculiarity of camp journalism when he wrote an article under the heading "Editor Annihilators."

This class of the genus-liped, almost wholly unknown in the Eastern States, flourishes . . . in the West. . . . An editor gives publicity to a current rumor on the street [and] the next morning in comes some overgrown mustached fellow and wants a "retraction." He publishes a letter reflecting ever so slightly on some individual— enter Mr. Man, and threatens blood and thunder, unless the thing is "made right." It is certainly wrong to criticize a man in a newspaper maliciously, but no matter how the case stands, the editor has to bear the brunt.[23]

Byers thought this mania for imagining affronts was confined to the southern and western states. He continued:

They go to law about it in the East which, on the whole, is probably the better way. And then, again, every little item is not noticed there as here. A good joke is laughed at, and forgotten. [But out West] it is brooded over until the meaning is so distorted that personality is seen sticking out of every line, and the fancied victim starts out with his friends to make a personal matter of it.[24]

Western editors were acutely aware of the tendency of readers to overreact and were prepared—if not willing—to meet opponents at any time. An Arizona editor perhaps spoke for all western journalists when he declared: "Recent developments go to show that to be a journalist in Arizona it is necessary to be a fighting man—a first-class bruiser—unless the editor would have his paper controlled by every demagogue who might feel disposed to dictate to him."[25]

Robert E. Fisk, brother of the Montana explorer and editor of the *Helena Weekly Herald,* demonstrated his considerable fighting abilities early in his journalistic career. After writing his first local for the *Herald,* Fisk was attacked by three town toughs who took exception to his article. In the encounter, Fisk gave a good account of himself. According to his younger brother, "he cleaned out the 'roughs' handsomely. Bob's face is scratched up some."[26] In the incident, however, it seems Fisk was not entirely blameless. When the case came to court, the judge found him guilty of assault and fined him twenty dollars and court costs.[27] Still, the two-fisted editor had no regrets. He wrote to his wife:

I have already had several difficulties in which I have sustained assault in my office and on the street, in each and all of which my assailants have come off second best. This peculiar and summary introduction to the public here, instead of doing me injury, has materially advanced me in the estimation of all good citizens, and myself and paper is backed today by the best and bravest men in the city.[28]

Some editors even seemed eager to take offense at criticism or stray remarks. A New Mexico editor warned his readers straight off that he belonged to the "church militant" and would "return 'good for evil;' that is, if you give us a knock, we will give you as good as we got. Draw it mild."[29]

One of the most controversial and colorful of the camp editors was Frederick J. Stanton. A native of England and well educated, Stanton no sooner arrived in Denver City when he became involved in an affair of honor with A. D. Richardson, a nationally-known correspondent for the *New York Tribune.* In a public card to Richardson, Stanton made a half-hearted attempt to assuage Richardson's wounded feelings, but he plainly warned that if the matter between them continued "we can measure off twenty paces. . . and show him that it is not the first time we have marked them off."[30] When Stanton became editor of the *Denver Daily Gazette* in 1865, he gained widespread notoriety for his trigger temper and readiness to respond to any criticism by physical violence. Ovando J. Hollister, editor of the *Daily Miners' Register* (Cental City, Colorado), became the target of Stanton's considerable editorial wrath when he innocently remarked that Stanton's *Gazette* appeared to be reduced in size. Stanton printed Hollister's remarks in full and then savagely replied:

The deep malignity of the vile scoundrel who wrote the above, equals only his audacity. His name is Hollister, which is, in his case, synonymous with everything low and degraded. A drunken debauchee in private, a liar, theive [sic] and common vagabond in public; he can claim nothing in common with his profession. We can only hope he will never cross our path in any way in society, or we will not be responsible for a personal chastisement he is bound to receive at our hands.[31]

This sensitivity to criticism was shared by many camp editors. They worked long and hard to make their product presentable; when their sheets were attacked for dullness or poor appearance, they took the rebukes personally. Some believed that it was "unmanly" to allow attacks to go unanswered, that camp residents would not support a paper if its editor were reluctant to respond to opponents. As a result, camp journalists often indulged in public disputes with their enemies— political opponents, town loafers, nonpaying subscribers, government officials, Indian agents, rival editors, to name only a few—arguments which began quietly enough, but which, because of the editors' zeal and impassioned rhetoric, frequently ended in physical violence.

One such affray was between General H. H. Heath and A. P. Sullivan, editor of the *Santa Fe Post*. After an absence of several years from New Mexico, Heath returned to Santa Fe where he secured a temporary position in the Office of the United States Assessor. Editor Sullivan, who wanted the job for himself, used the columns of the *Post* to discredit the general, branding him a "liar, coward, scoundrel and thief."[32] When the two men accidentally encountered each other in a Sante Fe store, Heath took the occasion to assualt Sullivan with his ivory-tipped cane. Sullivan managed to block most of the blows, but when Heath drew his gun, the unarmed editor beat a hasty retreat. Returning to his office, Sullivan collected a pair of revolvers and set off for Heath's residence. "As we approached the house," recounted Sullivan, "he opened fire with a carbine. We replied with our revolver, and were greeted with a second shot. . . ."[33] Before Sullivan could snap off another shot, the United States Marshal arrived and arrested the two men. Despite the seriousness of the affair and the excitement it aroused in Santa Fe, neither man was brought to trial and no legal action was taken against them. Apparently, the episode was quickly forgotten; certainly Sullivan's standing in the community did not suffer. One prominent resident, the wife of the secretary of New Mexico Territory, thought the brash Sullivan a "very fine young man who neither drinks, smokes, chews or has any bad habits."[34] Sullivan continued his editorial duties and remained with the *Post* for another five years.

In their zeal to protect their honor, camp editors often ignored legal niceties and publicly declared their willingness to settle disputes outside the courts, even on the "field of honor" if necessary. The editor of the *Madisonian* (Virginia City, Montana) was of the opinion that some personal disputes "do not always find their way into courts of justice" and that "sometimes the dexterous use of a pick handle" was necessary to show a man the error of his ways.[35] When Nathan A. Baker, editor of the *Cheyenne Leader*, wrote an unfriendly line about the ever-angry Frederick Stanton, the latter replied in his *Denver Daily Gazette* that Baker "must not name the family of Mr. Stanton in anyway, shape or manner, disrespectfully or otherwise, in the columns of a newspaper, unless he is prepared to take a personal responsibility the first time a meeting takes place between them."[36] Labelled a "debauched and debased coward and slanderer" by the editor of the *Tucson Citizen*, John Marion of the *Weekly Arizona Miner* (Prescott) angrily declared: "Mercy! Has it come to this? If so, we, the senior editor of this paper, unhesitantingly fling those words back into the teeth of this bluffing dog, and dare him to meet us at any place he may name, and forever settle this little matter of cowardice."[37] And in Deer Lodge, Montana, the editor of the *Weekly Independent* admitted that he had called one "Jaspor" a "liar and villain," and notified all that if "Jaspor" wanted "redress, we earnestly request of him, if he ever passes through Deer Lodge, to let us know of his presence here."[38]

While most western editors were loath to resort to such extralegal means of settling disputes, even the most law-abiding and temperate occasionally were driven to defend their honor by a resort to arms. William Byers, the recognized "dean" of mountain journalists, had once strongly denounced the practice of duelling: "To anyone," he had said, "who may feel like 'calling us out,' we have merely to remark that you will only waste your time. . . . You may murder us, but *never* on the so-called *field of honor* under the dignified name of a duel."[39] Yet two years later, Byers changed his tune and publicly challenged a neighboring editor and old acquaintance, Thomas Gibson, to a duel. Announcing in his paper that a "skunk must be driven away," Byers inserted a "personal card" addressed to Gibson: "Your card bearing date of yesterday, is before me. I must ask an explanation. If you mean by it a challenge to meet you on the ensanguined field, I prefer that your next note be by your 'friend'."[40] Again, in 1863, Byers felt it necessary to demand personal satisfaction. This time the dispute involved Ovando J. Hollister of the *Mining Journal* in Black Hawk, Colorado. Byers accused Hollister of willfully spreading slanderous lies about him and pointedly remarked that "we are going to nail this thing right here, or give Hollister a chance to nail us. Bring on your 'responsible man'."[41]

Challenges such as these were not made simply because camp editors were hot-tempered or spoiled for a good fight. They were far too involved with their community and its survival to lightly engage in any activity that might bring disgrace to the camp or create an unfavorable impression abroad. It was this very commitment to the camp that prompted them to defend their own honor with such vehemence. They believed that as the camp's most visible citizen it was their responsibility to answer reckless and malicious criticism quickly and in the strongest possible terms. When this criticism became personal, they interpreted it not only as an attack on their own character but also on the good name of the camp. If, in their opinion, the response necessarily meant a resort to arms, then they felt such a response was entirely justified and proper.

Their willingness to fight if necessary to defend the honor of the camp reflected the extent to which editors were involved in everyday affairs of the community. Much of this involvement was political. Nearly all were elected or appointed to important political positions in the camp and in the territory. Editors acted variously as mayors, delegates to Congress, postmasters, territorial secretaries, town treasurers, school superintendents, state and territorial auditors, and even as governors.[42] Indeed, many used their position as editor to springboard themselves into politics. W. R. Thomas of the Denver *Rocky Mountain News* revealed to his father that he was considering a career in politics and that he had a better than average chance of success since a "journalist will never lack opportunities for vengeance" against opponents.[43] Similarly, John P. Clum, editor of the *Arizona Citizen* (Tucson) and former Indian Agent of the San Carlos Apache Reservation, had designs of using his influence as editor to become governor of Arizona.[44] If editors did not covet political office for themselves, they often determined who would be appointed to choice offices. In a letter to Carl Schurz, secretary of the Interior in the Grant Administration, Robert Fisk of the *Helena Herald* strongly advised against the appointment of James Mills to the position of secretary of Montana. Fisk pointed out that Mills, editor of the *New North-West*, was closely allied with George M. Pinney, the "Boss Tweed" of the territory and notorious "killer" of Montana's ex-Governor Beall. Fisk's entreaty had its effect; Mills was never appointed to the position.[45]

Many editors also had a significant financial investment in the camp. Much of their available capital, of course, was tied up with the operation of the newspaper, but as the camp's news gatherer they had access to the latest progress in the mines and were privy to the secrets of real estate developers and business leaders. Armed with privileged information, many editors could not resist the temptation to invest whatever capital they possessed in various land and mining properties. Frank Hall was one of these opportunistic camp editors. By

1874, only a few years after he became a partner in the *Central City Miners' Register,* Hall owned properties in Central City, Colorado worth between $12,000 and $14,000, had a sizable interest in 560 acres of "good land in Southern Colorado through which a railroad is now being built,"[46] and had poured some six thousand dollars in eighty acres of land adjoining the rival town of Denver.[47] With financial holdings of this size and extent, editors were especially anxious to promote the camp—even when it was obvious to all that the diggings were petering out and the population was drifting away to other gulches. In Frank Hall's case, however, the effort was for naught. In 1878 he declared bankruptcy and was forced to abandon his properties and to sell his newspaper.[48] But to the end he gave unfailing encouragement to his fellow townsfolk, vigorously promoted the camp and in general defended western interests.[49]

Western journalists were keenly aware of the rise and fall of their fellow camp editors. In some instances the failure of a rival was occasion for joy and celebration. More often though, editors reacted sympathetically to the financial misfortunes of their "cotemporaries." Their common backgrounds, their shared experiences and their unflappable enthusiasm for the mining West created among them a sense of common purpose and a certain unity. As one Arizona editor said of a rival: "The Tucson *Citizen* has lived through two years, and started the third. Its editor and publisher [says] that the paper has neither brought him 'riches nor poverty.' Although, in the past, we have had some hot words with the *Citizen*, we freely acknowledge that it has accomplished much good for the Territory. . . ."[50] Despite all their infighting, their heated exchanges and press battles, editors willingly came to the defense of even their most bitter rivals. When William Byers was taken to task for his "plodding ways," O.J. Goldrick of the *Rocky Mountain Herald* (Denver) scolded those who would attack the "pioneer journalist of the Mining West." Calling his attackers ungrateful "struts" who wanted to put a "beard" on the venerable editor, he pointed out that Byers had braved the hardships and dangers of 1859 and had risked kidnapping and hanging to publish the *Rocky Mountain News.* Plainly irritated with Byers' critics, Goldrick grumbled: "Away with this cheap class of 'journalists', freshmen, bohemians, 'beats' or whatever they called 'em where they left."[51]

Even the most successful of camp editors had endured the "cuffs and snarls" of ungrateful subscribers; had experienced those initial days of unrest and uncertainty when with hat in hand they had humbly bowed to business and political leaders in an attempt to gain financial backing, only to come away, more often than not, with far less than was necessary to ensure the solvency of their paper. This never-ending search for financial security also united western editors. Finding dependable sources of revenue was for all of them the first—and for some—the last order of business.

3

The First
Order
of Business

Early western journalists may have possessed an abundance of enthusiasm and a deep sense of purpose, but they were chronically short of available cash. They invested small fortunes in printing presses, type, supplies, freight charges, rents, and labor and unless they could quickly exploit dependable sources of revenue, their journalistic careers were sure to be short-lived. The cost of a complete printing office varied according to size and the sophistication of the equipment, but throughout the frontier period even the most primitive averaged about $3,000.[1] Moreover, weekly operating costs were much higher in the Rocky Mountain mining West than in the East. A Colorado editor estimated that because of exorbitant freight rates the "cost of every article consumed is more than double the cost in the States. . . ."[2] In addition to various office expenditures, of course, publishers were responsible for paying the wages of employees. An editor's salary alone averaged forty dollars a week, while the going pay for experienced printers was about one hundred dollars a month.[3] With weekly payrolls often reaching five hundred dollars, it was essential that owners immediately establish reliable sources of income.

To most publishers, a promising source seemed to be the pocketbooks of the camp's potential subscribers. After all, as an eastern correspondent remarked, most westerners were "starved" for news and "no other nation so subsists upon the daily journals as our own."[4] There can be no doubt that mining camp residents craved reading materials. Even before beginning their journey West, goldseekers were warned about the scarcity of literature in the camps. The St. Louis *Daily Missouri Democrat* urged prospective emigrants to prepay their subscriptions to their favorite papers because the minimum price for any newspaper in the mining camps was thirty-five cents.

The *Democrat* further advised goldseekers to take their own books and magazines so that they would have something to read when they were not working.[5] A miner in Central City, Colorado, who failed to heed the advice, wrote home to his family saying that "we buy a weekly *Tribune* occasionally . . . to keep posted on the news. Every thing is readable these long nights and would give a pension *had I one to spare* for my text books. . . ."[6] In Virginia City, Montana, a pioneer woman complained that "I would give any thing imaginable, if I could spend about a week reading. . . . I have never read so little since I have known how to read as I have since I have been in Virginia [City]."[7] Finally, another Montana camp dweller who had suffered from the lonely nights remembered that "we read everything we could get hold of. There were but few books in the community, and these went the rounds of those who were fond of literature. Newspapers were several weeks old when they reached us; and we rarely saw magazines, though this was a trial for me."[8]

Aware of this literary thirst, editors were confident that they could find an immediate source of income through subscriptions. The enthusiastic reception accorded to camp journals seemed to justify this confidence, for the establishment of a community's first newspaper usually was the cause of celebration and much excitement. When the *Cheyenne Leader* issued its first edition a crowd of some three hundred besieged the paper's office and according to one witness "startled and often unique expressions were common from the lips of purchasers as they eagerly grasped the paper and witnessed the early and unexpected evidence of frontier enterprise."[9] A similar outpouring of jubilation occurred when the first printing office arrived in Missoula, Montana. The press had been hauled over the mountains from Helena, and when it reached Missoula the townsfolk declared a general holiday. A brass band accompanied the "press on wheels" as it made its triumphant entrance into town. The colorful displays of banners and flags throughout the camp prompted the teamsters to inquire whether the festivities were somehow connected with the Fourth of July.[10]

Demonstrations of support were encouraging, but of far greater importance to the editors was the financial commitment residents were willing to extend to the paper. In the beginning they had reason to be optimistic. Single copies were purchased almost as quickly as they could be printed. One Colorado editor, delighted by the warm reception he had received, scrawled in his diary that "papers go like hot cakes" and that he was sorely tested to keep up with the demand.[11] Mary Edgerton, the wife of the governor of Montana, made the same observation. Writing to her sister from Bannack, she noted that she received copies of the *Montana Post* from her husband in Virginia City, but she could read them only "if I can keep them! There are so few that they are used up pretty fast."[12]

Camp journalists, however, were not lulled into complacency by the initial enthusiastic response nor did they take for granted the financial support of local residents. Selling single copies was one matter; obtaining long term subscriptions quite another. Miners were occasionally willing to buy the paper, but some were reluctant to subscribe on a yearly or monthly basis. In the first place, many were loyal to hometown or eastern journals and preferred to spend what little money they had on these familiar sheets. Commonly read in the camps were papers such as the *Leavenworth Times, St. Louis Republican, St. Louis Democrat, New York Tribune, Washington Chronicle, Harper's Weekly*, and the *American Journal of Mining*.[13] These established papers contained far more reading material and even though they arrived weeks and months after they were published, they were avidly read by camp residents, often to the exclusion of the camp paper. Further, the high asking price for camp papers disturbed many residents. A year's subscription could run as high as twelve dollars, although the average annual cost for a weekly was between three and seven dollars.[14] Because editors wanted subscriptions paid for in advance, many miners simply could not afford to subscribe. Finally, most goldseekers had no idea how long they would remain in any given camp. In a sense all mining communities were "turnstile towns,"[15] settlements where the ebb and flow of people was continuous. To ask residents to subscribe and to pay for that subscription in advance was asking more than many were willing to commit themselves to.

Nevertheless, editors did their best to convince camp dwellers that it was in their interest to support generously their local paper. They argued that it was the westerners' responsibility, their civic duty, to lend financial assistance. The *Rocky Mountain News* came straight to the point and bluntly told readers that "private citizens of Denver and the Mountains will realize their responsibilities to their press, and respond in subscription patronage. . . . It is the privilege, as it ought to be the understood obligation, of the valley and mountain reader to patronize the enterprise of supplying them with the latest news. . . ."[16]

The most common argument advanced for the need to support camp papers was that through them the outside world learned of the greatness of the mining West; that the camp paper induced immigration and needed outside capital. According to one editor, by supporting the local paper residents "would help themselves and their neighbors to more advantage than twenty times the amount invested in grand streetcars, or chambers of commerce, stylish saloons, or even churches. The newspaper is calculated to enhance the value of property, induce immigration, give character to a country abroad, and be beneficial about home."[17]

Not only did editors advance nearly every possible argument to win the support of residents, but some also took extraordinary measures to round up subscribers. In New Mexico, the well-traveled *Cimarron News*[18] went so far as to employ the long arm of the law. The *News* announced that Sheriff Turner was soon leaving on a tax-collection excursion to the various districts surrounding Cimarron. It went on to report that the sheriff "has kindly consented to receive subscriptions to the *News* for us, while in such portions of the country which we are unable to visit. Such subscriptions will be duly acknowledged."[19]

Subscriptions, however, did not prove to be the financial bonanza expected. The most vexing problem concerned delinquent subscribers. Although subscriptions were to be paid "invariably in advance," editors often accepted partial payment with a promise that the balance would be paid at an agreed time. When payment came due, far too often the subscriber had moved on. To this class of delinquent the *Rocky Mountain News* in Denver gave this ruefull farewell:

And now, gentlemen—patrons—we must bid you a long—we fear last—farewell . . . and in doing so, permit us to remark that if at any time in your lives—even at a remote period in "your journey through this vale of tears," "this cold unfriendly world," thou should be smitten with remorse of conscience for having deceived the printer, and diddled him out of one or more dollars, be kind enough to contribute the sum to the "Mount Vernon Fund," "Washington Monument," . . . or any other charitable fund which may be fashionable at that remote day, send us receipt for the same, and we will . . . inscribe your name on the roll of honor.[20]

To the *Grant County Herald* the most annoying delinquents were those who signed up out of "pity" for the printer and then, when presented with the bill, claimed that they had subscribed for only three months instead of a year. Then there were those, said the

Herald, who had a "vague notion" that they owed "something," but did not think it important to pay on time.[21]

Several techniques were used to collect delinquent accounts. The most common was a simple editorial message. Delinquents were asked to pay up and all readers were warned that unless the money could be collected the paper was sure to fail. The message was usually couched in homey, even humorous language; its intent was to win over delinquents by friendly persuasion. When this method failed then more drastic measures were tried. "Delinquents" now were referred to editorially as "deadbeats" or "contemptible villains," and lengthy articles appeared warning them that there were severe legal penalties for defrauding the printer. Finally, those editors who had the manpower did not hesitate to send the more burly members of their staff on a house-to-house collection search.[22]

When all else failed, editors sometimes resorted to the practice of publishing "black lists" naming delinquent subscribers. On the frontier, however, public dunning often provoked a violent and dangerous response, and many journalists were reluctant to use the tactic. One declared that if he were to dun a reader "we might get a score or two of canings, or other abuse from its publication."[23] When William Byers of the *Rocky Mountain News* printed a "deadbeat list," an irate delinquent challenged him to a duel and called for a general meeting of the camp to "devise means of redress" for the "public wrong."[24] The affair finally came to a peaceful settlement, but thereafter Byers was extremely cautious about publishing the names of delinquent subscribers in his columns.[25] Despite the danger, most camp editors felt compelled to occasionally print the names of errant subscribers. They lost thousands of dollars yearly through unpaid bills and as the Deer Lodge, Montana, *New North-West* put it: "Self-preservation is the first law of nature."[26]

Subscribers also proved to be a sensitive and fickle lot. Should a news item, no matter how trivial, displease them or should they disagree with the paper's stand on a given issue, they were only too ready to cancel their subscription. For newly established papers, cancellations were particularly serious and editors took special pains to win back disgruntled readers. "If you do not agree with the *Pioneer,*" pleaded a Montana editor, "give us your dissenting opinions, and we will publish them in full. . . .But do not . . . stop your paper, for we might have to suspend publication of the *Pioneer* entirely, if you withdraw your patronage, and that would be a calamity to the whole country. . . ."[27] Editors bitterly complained about "ungrateful" readers who went about the camp urging fellow residents to stop the paper, and they let it be known that those who cancelled their subscriptions were directly attacking the welfare and good name of the community.

With the problems of collections and cancellations, it soon became apparent that revenue from subscriptions alone could not ensure the survival of any newspaper. In fact, of the major sources of income, subscriptions proved to be the least reliable. Without advertising and job work, declared Colorado's *Tri-Weekly Miners' Register*, "not one paper in a thousand could sustain itself. To pay the expenses of publishing this paper, if subscribers alone were relied on, would require between 800 and 1,000."[28] Although aware of this, editors continued their efforts to expand circulation, for any paper that could boast of a large readership was likely to receive valuable financial assistance from merchants and businessmen. This fact led some papers to make exaggerated circulation claims. In New Mexico the struggling *Grant County Herald* claimed an annual circulation of 75,000 and asserted that copies of that journal could be found in "every state of the Union."[29] The neighboring *Mesilla Times*, a financially troubled sheet operating at a loss, proudly announced a weekly circulation of 7,500, an impossibly high figure.[30]

In truth, a circulation of several hundred was respectable. Subscriptions for newly founded sheets seldom rose above one hundred, and editors relied principally on sales from single issues for revenue-producing income. In view of the limited journalistic market in the mountain West, this is not surprising. As a contemporary observer recalled, the average Wyoming newspaperman could view the limits of his business from the roof of his office.[31] Henry Blake, one of the first editors of the *Montana Post* (Virginia City), remembered that during the paper's first year, subscriptions were confined within the narrow boundaries of Alder Gulch and that it was difficult to gain long-term support from distant readers.[32] Once a paper managed to survive the first year, however, subscriptions usually increased dramatically. The *Weekly Arizona Miner* (Prescott) began with less than seventy-five subscribers, but within several years the number increased to nearly seven hundred; [33] in Virginia City, *The Montanian* expanded its circulation to well over a thousand;[34] and in Denver, after two years of operation, the *Daily Rocky Mountain News* claimed 550 subscribers.[35] Eventually, the more prominent camp papers enjoyed a relatively large circulation. The editor of *The Montanian* estimated that the two papers published in Helena alone annually reached 832,000 readers and placed the combined yearly circulation of all Montana papers at 1,084,000.[36]

Circulation claims such as these gave editors an entry into a more dependable source of income—advertising. Just as with subscribers, editors made a concerted effort to woo merchants and to convince them that the camp paper was the best medium through which to advertise their wares. They pointed to the paper's large home circulation and to the fact that it was sent to all parts of the country where "we are read with avidity, by thousands of persons who have friends here, or who contemplate removing hither."[37] Businessmen were told that a lively camp paper gave outward evidence that the community was thriving and its future secure. *The Rocky Mountain Gold Reporter* of Mountain City, Colorado, asserted that "advertising goes further to show the progress of a place than any other means" and that it was the obvious responsibility of the business community to see to it that the local newssheet was generously supported.[38] So important a source of income was advertising that editors were not above using intimidation as a means of gaining the support they believed was rightly theirs. Merchants who refused to patronize the paper were publicly "black listed," and residents were urged in the strongest terms to support only those businessmen who were "civic-minded." "Right here in our town," fumed the *Laramie Daily Sentinel*, "there are men trying to do business whose existence is scarcely known because they do not keep themselves before the public through the press, and such men ought to be ignored."[39] Denver's *Weekly Commonwealth* went so far as to question the business ethics of nonadvertisers: "When you see a man who is too close and stingy to advertise, you can safely put him down as being too selfish to deal generously or very fairly or honestly."[40]

By these and other methods, camp papers usually managed to gain merchant support. The columns of successful journals were crowded with advertisements of all kinds—a fact editors pointed to with pride. "There is something inspiring and cheerful, encouraging and hopeful, in the very look of well-filled advertising columns," crowed one editor. To this happy scribe, the men who succeed best in business "and keep up with the times are those who not only read the advertising columns diligently, but who do their share in keeping them 'ever charming, ever new'."[41]

Merchants also supported their local paper by outright cash contributions. *The Mesilla Times* editorially thanked one local merchant for
contributing $150 for one subscription and then asked, "Who will do
likewise?"[42] In some mining communities, businessmen actually sub-
sidized the paper. Andrew Fisk, part owner of *The Helena Herald*,
recalled that he and his brothers borrowed over $5,000 from Helena
merchants when they founded their paper; for the next six months,
only the cash donations from the camp's merchants prevented the
Herald from failing.[43] The Fisk's experience was by no means unique;
indeed, camp editors not only demanded but fully expected the financial assistance of local merchants. The *Rocky Mountain News* reported that it cost some $1,200 a week to operate the paper and it
forewarned merchants that they would be asked to contribute at least
$6.50 a week to help defray the high operating cost.[44]

Businessmen who were generous did not go unrewarded. Editors
took every opportunity to praise the establishments of large contribu-
tors and to remark editorially on their enterprise and community
spirit. In a serious discussion on Colorado hotels, the *Boulder County
Pioneer* took time to comment favorably on a particular boarding
house:

We have fared well and ill at nearly all the public houses in Colorado, and
regard for truth impels us to say that George [Squire] is the most accommo-
dating host in the Territory. He don't do anything by halves, and the Boulder House . . . is bound to remain a first-class institution . . . regardless of
profit or expense.[45]

But even the most grateful editor soon tired of the fine art of
puffing. One complained that editors in the West "must be enthusiastic on the subject of hams, verbose in extolling hardware, and highly
imaginative in the matter of dry goods . . . , be ecstatic and eloquent
on behalf of fat women, and of living skeletons."[46] Readers, too, tired
of the practice. A British traveler who had stopped in Denver remarked that the town's papers were "filled with puffs of quacks and
whiskey-shops."[47] Fearful of the unfavorable impression these inces-
sant puffs might have on distant readers, many editors called upon
their "cotemporaries" to discontinue them. *The Missoula Pioneer* was
one of the first mountain papers to declare openly that it would no
longer give space to unsolicited advertising and called upon other
Montana papers to follow a similar policy:

When, eh, when will our cotemporaries [sic] abstain from the publication of paltry, cock-robin compliments to their patrons? An outsider would infer from this newspaporial "puffing" that advertisers in Montana do not receive a fair equivalent for their money . . . . Let this reprehensible practice cease or we will say something.[48]

The pressing need for quick and ready cash forced most camp editors to accept nearly every kind of advertisement, and few troubled themselves to verify the claims of their patrons. Advertisements claiming magical cures, for example, appeared in the early camp press. One such advertisement read: "To all who are suffering from the errors and indiscretions of youth, nervous weakness, early decay, loss of manhood, etc., I will send a recipe that will cure you. . . . This great remedy was discovered by a missionary in South America." To receive this miraculous remedy, readers were to send their money to an address in New York City. [49] The gullible—or the very anxious— were not the only victims of fraudulent advertising. After running a series of announcements for a nonexistent New York insurance firm, the *Helena Herald* hotly denounced the company as a "consumate imposter" and warned readers and even rival papers not to patronize it.[50] Experience caused editors to be cautious about transacting business with distant or unknown companies, and most required cash in advance before allowing them advertising space.

Advertisements for saloon and gambling houses also were prominently displayed in frontier sheets. For many papers, the revenue from gambling and related establishments was significant, and editors frequently struck up close friendships with barkeepers and casino operators. One editor, after receiving a complimentary bottle of brandy from a nearby "watering spa," expressed his heartfelt thanks by urging readers to "go to the Saratoga for your drinks, and take a peep at the 'pretty waiter' girls."[51] But as the camp slowly began to attain an air of respectability, such open support became less conspicuous. In Colorado a rare teetotalling editor went to the extent of banning what he regarded as unsavory advertisements altogether. "Henceforth," he righteously proclaimed, "no whiskey, quack abortionist, lottery swindle, gambling device, or in fact any advertisement or announcement, large or small, whether it pays much or little, that savors in the least of illegality or swindling, shall find a place in these columns while we control them."[52] Most, however, did not go so far; instead, they simply refrained from endorsing drinking and gambling establishments or giving them undue attention.

The revenue gained through job printing was another important source of income. Even the smallest print shop prided itself on the variety of printing work it was equipped to perform and on the fancy type available to merchants and camp residents. When not occupied with issuing the daily or weekly paper, editors busied themselves by printing business cards, office letterheads and envelopes, theater tickets, restaurant menus, posters and broadsides, and a host of other printing orders. Some papers also took on the ambitious task of publishing full-length books. While still in Virginia City, the *Montana Post* published Thomas J. Dimsdale's epic history, *The Vigilantes of Montana; Or Popular Justice in the Rocky Mountains* (1866), the first book printed in the Territory of Montana; and the *Rocky Mountain News* published Julius E. Wharton's *History of the City of Denver from its Earliest Settlement to the Present Time* (1866), one of the earliest histories of Denver and its environs.[53]

Income generated by job work was nearly equal to that of advertising,[54] but some editors were less than exacting about establishing fixed prices for the work they performed. A business associate of E. A. Slack, editor of the Wyoming *South Pass News*, recalled that Slack was anything but "methodical" when it came to bookkeeping. "He used to say that one's guess was better than one's figures, and this was the way he reached prices upon job work. He never had such a thing as a cost system about his printing office and approximated everything."[55] This might be sufficient for small camp papers, but large ones could not afford to approximate anything. Not only did most editors keep detailed financial records, but they also were keenly aware of the merchants who transacted business with them. Again, when they found evidence that local businessmen were sending their job work to the East, they publicly called attention to it and urged residents not to patronize these "traitors to the community."[56] Using the familiar argument that it was the solemn duty and responsibility of merchants to support home institutions, they reminded their readers that unless the paper received proper support it was bound to fail, an event that would seriously damage the image and welfare of the community.

Profits from subscriptions, advertising, and job printing were the principal sources of income for most camp papers. Some also depended upon government printing to meet operating expenses. Indeed, the income derived from the right to print the official post office letter list, government patents and land sales, the minutes of

town council meetings and territorial legislatures, and other government documents was for some papers the sole source of dependable
revenue. Of course, it was in the interest of every camp paper to
obtain the government contract and all made a determined effort to
secure it.[57] When his bitter rival, James H. Mills, was awarded the
federal printing contract, Robert Fisk of the *Helena Herald* approached
Montana Governor B. F. Potts and asked him to use his influence in
Washington, D.C., to return the contract to the *Herald*. Potts, who
had received many favors from Fisk through the *Herald,* agreed and
in a letter to a high-ranking official he sharply attacked editor Mills:
"James H. Mills has been enabled to purchase the materials for his
newspaper by the patronage of the federal offices in Virginia City, and
now for nearly a year he has been throwing mud at the Administration. He abused you soundly last spring. . . . Mills is run by Hiram
Knowles, one of our judges, who approved Mills' course and is his
counsellor." Potts went on the argue that Fisk, as a loyal administration man, deserved the public printing.[58] Through Potts' intervention
Fisk eventually won the contract, and Mills was forced to rely on
other sources of income. Other papers did not have the luxury of
losing such a battle—without government patronage they would die.
The editor of the Helena *Rocky Mountain Gazette* minced no words:
"I trust I do not exaggerate matters when I state that the existence of
the *Gazette* depends upon securing it [the government contract].
How we are to get along from January to May next without it I cannot
imagine."[59]

Receiving government patronage depended on the paper's political
leanings, yet most camp sheets were founded without any announced
party allegiance. Editors instead pledged to be "Independent in all
things, but neutral in nothing which interests the public,"[60] and promised to attend strictly to "local issues." They took this middle road in
part because they believed that political discussions were out of place
in the mining West, or as one Colorado miner put it: "I hear nothing
about politics out here as every body is for money and not for office. . . ."[61] Editors also eschewed partisan politics because they were
fearful of antagonizing a significant segment of the camp's population.
Should important merchants and camp leaders take exception to the
paper's political philosophy and consequently refuse to lend it financial support, it would be difficult to gain widespread approval in the
camp. Most mountain papers, therefore, initially avoided controversial discussions and concentrated on advancing the economic and

cultural interests of the camp. One typically cautious editor justified his neutral position by opining that:

a political paper has no business in Montana, anyhow—the advancement of rail-road, wagon-road and telegraph facilities . . . , improved postal facilities, the encouragement of agriculture, fostering educational facilities, inducing immigration, these . . . have stronger claim upon brains and printer's ink than the old hackneyed arguments and long stereotyped phraseology of petty party politics, that attract the attention of people in the East for want of something more interesting and exciting.[62]

For all their protestations of neutrality, it was nevertheless difficult for camp editors to refrain long from entering partisan debates or openly declaring allegiance to a political party. Some took this step out of economic necessity. By vigorously supporting one party, some editors believed that the paper would immediately receive the overwhelming financial backing of the party's faithful. Thus, the *Denver Daily Gazette*, an organ of the Democratic party, demanded of every follower of The Democracy, to "Make it his business to go around amongst his neighbors and friends and persuade them to subscribe for the *Gazette*. Remember, by so doing . . . you just so much add to your influence . . . and strengthen the hands of your fellow Democrats."[63] For some papers this tactic worked—for others it was a disaster. The editor of the *Colorado Miner* (Georgetown) confessed that he had thought enough Republican voters were in Georgetown to sustain the paper, but he was forced to admit that his political stand had been a "fatal mistake" and announced his return to an independent position.[64]

Despite this initial reluctance, the pressure of territorial politics and the prospect of gaining yet another source of income caused nearly all the papers eventually to endorse a particular political party or group. When they did, they were not slow to seek their reward. Editor E. S. Wilkinson of the Helena, Montana *Rocky Mounain Gazette* reminded Martin Maginnis, a candidate for Montana's delegate to Congress, that a contribution of five hundred dollars to the paper would "be an additional inducement to aid you in getting the next nomination, and also aid us in starting business."[65] The Fisk brothers, too, lost no time in making the rounds of Helena's sizable Republican population. A few weeks following the *Herald*'s founding, Andrew J. Fisk noted in his diary that "the Republicans are doing nobly for Bob [Fisk]—about $15,000 has been raised already—only want $300 more."[66] Strong-arm methods to secure patronage, however, sometimes backfired. When P. W. Dooner, editor of the Tucson *Weekly Arizonan* attempted to solicit a $3,000 contribution from Richard C. McCormick, McCormick angrily reacted by buying his own newspaper, the *Arizona Citizen*, an action that caused the demise of the *Arizonan*.[67]

On the other hand, when political leaders made a sizable contribution to a paper, they expected a fair return on their investment. Most were not disappointed. Editors waxed eloquently on the attributes and qualifications of their benefactors and worked tirelessly in their behalf. During campaigns they were particularly active and took every opportunity to explain the positions of their favorites and expose the errors of opponents. Readers were bombarded by a bewildering array of political invective, and campaign items often crowded out everyday news and even advertising space. When the excitement of the race had passed, editors were always ready to stand by their patrons. As J. B. Chaffee, Colorado's delegate to Congress confidently expressed to one editor: "I know you and the *Register* [Central City] will do your part."[68]

When their personal candidate won political office, camp editors were generously rewarded. William Clagett, Montana's delegate to Congress, displayed his appreciation for editor Robert Fisk's support by appointing Fisk's brother to the post of collector of customs, a position that, according to Clagett, would be worth some $1,200 every year to the *Herald*.[69] Income from government printing was also considerable. Papers that received the contract could expect to gain from $3,500 to $5,000 annually, amounts that often were fully one-fourth the paper's total income.[70]

Although editors freely admitted their political affiliations, they hotly denied that they were in any way "bought or sold" and claimed full freedom of editorial expression. William Byers, long a staunch Republican and a known champion of Colorado's territorial governor, John Evans, strongly objected when his *Rocky Mountain News* was accused of being the "organ" of the Evans' faction. "The *News* is not the organ of Governor Evans," he declared,

nor of any other man or set of men save and except John L. Dailey and the writer of this, who is its sole and exclusive owners and managers. Gov. Evans never owned a dollar interest in the establishment, never attempted to dictate what it should say and could not if he would, and is not in the remotest degree responsible for anything published in its columns.[71]

Whether Byers received any direct financial backing from the Evans group is impossible to determine; however, Byers had long allied himself with Evans and received his share of choice political appointments and government printing contracts. Certainly, Byers and Evans were of one mind when it came to Colorado territorial politics and the two shared many business interests.[72]

Only a few camp papers escaped the mad scramble for financial security. *The Arizonian,* founded in Tubac in 1859 and published irregularly until 1870, was owned and generously supported by two mining companies, the Sonora Exploring and Mining Company and the Santa Rita Silver Mining Company. Both wanted to stimulate mining activity in southern Arizona and used the columns of the *Arizonian* to excite the attention of eastern capitalists.[73] It also is likely that the *Arizonian* received some subvention from the Texas Railroad Company,[74] which was interested in promoting settlement in Arizona. Between 1870 and 1874, the *Cimarron News and Press* (New Mexico) was owned and operated by the Maxwell Land Grant and Railway Company. The agreement between the company and its chosen editor, Alexander P. Sullivan, specified that Sullivan was to

publish at [Cimarron] a twenty-four column weekly newspaper . . . to be printed on clear white paper . . . with good clear and legible type [and] said newspaper to be devoted particularly to advancing the interest of said Maxwell Land Grant and Railway Company . . . and aid in the development of the resources of its property and the resources of Northern New Mexico.[75]

To free Sullivan from any financial worries, the Company agreed to

guarantee him a subscription of Five Hundred copies to said Newspaper at the rate of five dollars for each copy to be paid as follows, twelve hundred dollars . . . at once, five hundred dollars at the end of three months and the remaining eight hundred at the end of six months. . . .[76]

Four years later when the land company sold out, the new owner quickly informed readers that "hitherto it has been necessary for the *News* to rely upon resources outside of its legitimate income, but now it has no subsidy to back it (which may be unfortunate), and must now derive its support from its patrons. It is undertaken, experimentally, and as its support is, so shall the paper be."[77] But company-backed papers, no matter how lucrative to money-poor editors, were rare in the mining West, and those that were founded usually were short-lived.

Editors had varying degrees of success in their frantic search for financial stability. The *Arizonian* in Tubac lived only a few months and a similar fate befell the *Caribou Post* (Colorado), the *Moreno Lantern* (Elizabethtown, New Mexico), *South Pass News* and *The Sweetwater Mines* (South Pass City, Wyoming), *Canon City Times* (Colorado), and the *Mesila Times* (New Mexico). Even in those communities where the mines remained productive, many papers failed.[78] Like the editors, camp residents often did not have ready cash to spend. One mountain editor who was forced to suspend operations explained that his neighbors were "poor in money and rich in property, and those who have desired have received the paper without pay, until such time as they could conveniently spare it. To us this has been a losing business. . . ."[79] Other reasons, too, caused newspaper failures. Much depended on the editor's skill with a pen and his ability to win the good will of his fellows. Ovando J. Hollister of the Black Hawk *Daily Mining Journal* thought his unqualified "adhersion to the Republican Party" caused the demise of his paper,[80] while P. W. Dooner, of the Tucson *Weekly Arizonan*, blamed his own "unworthiness."[81] Editors also had to possess sound business sense to operate successfully their sheets, and many failed through their own financial incompetence. John Wasson of the Tucson *Arizona Citizen* thought good business sense the most important factor in any newspaper's success, and "the business of publishing a newspaper can only be maintained by observing those principles by which merchants, mechanics, farmers and professional men of sense are governed."[82]

In spite of the continuous effort to tap dependable sources of revenue, few camp papers operated at more than a modest profit. Noting the difficulties of editing a newspaper on the frontier, a pioneer journalist observed that "small population and magnificent distances made their financial lot difficult, but they did not complain and . . . gave the reader more than warranted by the patronage. No Wyoming newspaperman has made a fortune in the business. A few have accumulated a small competence. . . ."[83] In most cases, what profits there were went to the purchase of new equipment and the construction of more modern offices. Editor Wasson estimated that over a five year period his paper had netted only $9,000 and declared that "what profit it has made for the proprietor has been expended in adding new material to the office."[84] The money editors poured into improvements was considerable. The Fisk brothers spent over $60,000 to build a "fire-proof" office, which then burned to the ground two years after completion.[85] Frank Hall of the Central City *Miners' Register* was forever buying new presses in a futile attempt to keep pace with the Denver papers.[86] Perhaps John L. Dailey stated it best when he said that nearly every penny he and his partner William Byers earned from the *Rocky Mountain News* went back into the paper. "Byers made more money by his land than anything else. We put up a building, saved a little, and put everything we could into the paper to improve."[87]

Even though the camp press functioned in a limited and highly confined journalistic market, editors felt compelled to improve their product by the force of the competition. Many camps witnessed the founding of not one paper but several. Only a year following the Rush of 1859 four newspapers competed for the affection and financial backing of Denver City residents; South Pass City, Wyoming, with only a population of three thousand, had two newspapers, both of which failed within a few months; and in Helena, Montana, several newspapers operated simultaneously during the frontier period. As a result, editors spent large sums on improving the appearance of their papers, in purchasing new presses and more decorative type—all to force their rivals from the field of battle. While they had real affection for one another, the serious struggle for survival caused them to have less than cordial professional relationships with what they called their "cotemporaries."

Washington hand press, the usual equipment of a frontier newspaper. (Arizona Historical Society.)

Editor William N. Byers of Denver's *Rocky Mountain News* hoped to keep peace with the rival towns of Auraria and Denver City, located on opposite banks of Cherry Creek, by placing his print shop in the middle of the creek bed. (Denver Public Library, Western History Department.)

The trickle of water called Cherry Creek became a torrent in the spring of 1864. The *Commonwealth* office survived, but it was quickly purchased by the enterprising editor of the *Rocky Mountain News*, thus ending one of the longest and most bitter of all boom town newspaper wars. (Denver Public Library, Western History Department.)

ROCKY MOUNTAIN NEWS.

VOL. 1. CHERRY CREEK, K. T., SATURDAY, APRIL 23 1859. NO. 1.

The first issue of the *Rocky Mountain News*, dated April 23, 1859, but actually distributed to an excited populace the evening before. (Denver Public Library, Western History Department.)

Numerous threats from outraged readers and one nearly successful kidnap and hanging attempt prompted editor William N. Byers to arm his small staff of assistants at the *Rocky Mountain News*. (Denver Public Library, Western History Department.)

William N. Byers, editor of the *Rocky Mountain News*, in well-deserved retirement. (Denver Public Library, Western History Department.)

O. J. Goldrick, Colorado's first school teacher and editor of papers in Denver, Black Hawk, and Central City. Goldrick confounded early Denver residents with his fluency in Latin and Greek, languages the miners thought were "tribe talk." (Denver Public Library, Western History Department.)

Frank Hall, secretary of Colorado and often acting territorial governor, was editor of papers in Black Hawk and Central City, Colorado. (Denver Public Library, Western History Department.)

John L. Dailey was the steady hand behind the success of Denver's *Rocky Mountain News*, but his contributions were overshadowed by his more aggressive and colorful partner, William N. Byers. (Denver Public Library, Western History Department.)

The hasty-construction characteristic of boom towns is seen in this view of Central City, Colorado, in 1863. (Denver Public Library, Western History Department.)

OFFICE OF

Colorado Miner,

GEORGETOWN, COLORADO.

Dear Sir:

The time for which the MINER *to your address has been paid, will expire in one month; see date on printed address. Shall we continue the paper? We can promise that it shall be fully up to the standard of the past year, end we hope to make it even more worthy of your patronage. As we prepay the postage without adding the amount to the subscription price, it is the same as deducting it from it; so that while you will be getting a better paper, it will not cost you as much as usual.*

Yours, with great respect,

Cree & Patterson

Boom town newspapers made frequent pleas for the support of town residents. This one, in fancy type, was one of the more dignified. (Denver Public Library, Western History Department.)

50

The Central City, Colorado, *Mining Register*, edited by Frank Hall and David Collier, was one boom town newspaper that made it through the difficult early years. (Denver Public Library, Western History Department.)

South Pass City, Wyoming,
during its boom days.
(Denver Public Library,
Western History Depart-
ment.)

Nathan A. Baker, editor of
the first three papers
published in Wyoming
Territory. Baker got his start
in frontier journalism as a
compositor on the staff of
Denver's *Rocky Mountain
News*. (Denver Public
Library, Western History
Department.)

Elizabethtown, first incorporated town in New Mexico Territory and seen here in its declining years, went from boom to bust between 1867 and 1875. Its residents were briefly provided news by the *Moreno Lantern*, a paper that would be forced to depart for better journalistic markets. (State Records Center and Archives, Santa Fe.)

John Wasson, pioneer editor of the Tucson *Arizona Citizen*. (Arizona Historical Society.)

Opposite, above. The Tucson *Arizona Citizen* located its first office above the bar in the Congress Hall Saloon. (Arizona Historical Society.)

Opposite, below. The *Arizona Citizen* survived the initial hell days in Tucson and moved to bigger and better offices by the 1890s. (Arizona Historical Society.)

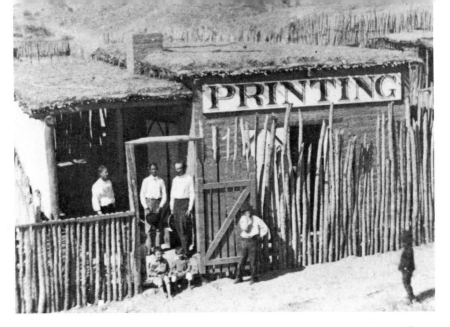

The Tubac *Arizonian* office was typical of the frontier boom town buildings that housed newspapers. (Arizona Historical Society.)

Colorful John P. Clum (center), editor and founder of the *Tombstone Epitaph* (Arizona). (Denver Public Library, Western History Department.)

James H. Mills, as editor of the *Montana Post* after its removal from Virginia City to Helena, lost his battle against the *Helena Herald*. Later Mills found journalistic success with the *New North-West* in Deer Lodge, Montana. (Montana Historical Society, Helena.)

Deer Lodge, Montana Territory, where James H. Mills established the *New North-West* as a powerful force in Montana politics. (Montana Historical Society, Helena.)

Robert E. Fisk, the two-fisted founder of the *Helena Herald.* Following the first issue of the *Herald,* several "town toughs" took exception to an article Fisk wrote and attacked him on the street, but the would-be assailants were beaten back by the editor. (Montana Historical Society, Helena.)

Thomas Dimsdale, pioneer editor of the *Montana Post* in Virginia City. Dimsdale's epic classic, *The Vigilantes of Montana,* the first book published in the Territory of Montana, was serialized in the *Post.* (Montana Historical Society, Helena.)

The office of the *Montana Post* and City Book Store in Virginia City in 1867, three years after the founding of the newspaper. (Montana Historical Society, Helena.)

Office of the prosperous *Helena Herald,* the winner of a brisk newspaper war with the *Montana Post* and two other rivals. (Montana Historical Society, Helena.)

Below: Main street of Helena, Montana, in 1872—a boom town well on its way to permanence. (Montana Historical Society, Helena.)

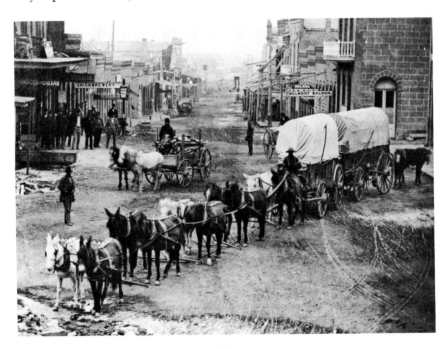

4

Battling
"Cotemporaries"

In splendid isolation as Montana's only newspaper, Virginia City's *Montana Post* took time in the late spring of 1865 to survey the western journalistic scene. Its nearest "cotemporary,"[1] the *Rocky Mountain News*, was located some 950 miles to the south, at the junction of Cherry Creek and the South Platte River in Denver, Colorado Territory. The *Post* had only kind words for what it called the "pioneer journal of the Mountains," and wished the *News* a long, healthy, and properous career. Fully aware of the risks of founding and operating a territory's first newspaper, the *Post* praised the distant editors for their honesty, ability, and fearlessness and called attention to the high standing and wide circulation that their paper enjoyed throughout the mountain west. The *Post* concluded its affectionate review by acknowledging that "one flag shelters us both and we shake hands on politics, these days."[2] Several years later, after the *Post* pulled out of Alder Gulch and moved to Last Chance Gulch in the booming camp of Helena, the *Rocky Mountain Herald* in Denver took note of the move by declaring that "the *Post* is now, and has been for many years past, perhaps the best newspaper in the west—except the *Sacramento Union*."[3]

When vast distances of unoccupied mountain and plains separated camp newspapers and when they operated entirely independently of each other, such expressions of mutual affection and respect were common. Even at closer range, if the papers competed in separate journalistic markets and did not pose an economic threat to one another, a spirit of cooperation often prevailed between them. Thus, the *New North-West* in Deer Lodge, Montana, a staunch Republican sheet, could speak well of its Democratic rival, the *Rocky Mountain Gazette* of nearby Helena. Reporting that the *Gazette*'s printing plant had been severely damaged by fire, the *New North-West* avowed that:

since its establishment in '66 the *Gazette* has been one of the leading papers of the West and Northwest. It has endeavored to build up the Territory to that standard its great resources will warrant. There has been no nook or corner, nor place so far out of the way in our mountains, where civilized man dwelt, that it did not find. And although destroyed, it will rise up again.[4]

Any editorial sparring between these relatively financially secure sheets appeared in the form of friendly banter and good-natured jousting. One editor announced in his "Salutatory" that he expected to have a "jolly, old row with our hardworking, good looking cotemps across the way" but promised not to "fire on the picket line, or infringe on the rules of civilized warfare. . . ."[5] Editors frequently displayed their friendly intentions by loaning paper and other essential supplies to their neighbors. When the entire office of the *Rocky Mountain News* was swept away by the Cherry Creek flood of 1864, Simon Whiteley, editor of Denver's *Daily Commonwealth*, extended every courtesy to the paper and allowed issues of the *News* to be printed on *Commonwealth* presses.[6]

Despite these and other gestures of good will, many editors anticipated trouble with their western contemporaries. Upon assuming the editorial controls of the *Rocky Mountain News*, Ovando J. Hollister, a survivor of many journalistic wars, was quick to pen a message to his fellow editors. Pointing out that he had always tried to avoid "Personal discussions" in public, he expressed the hope that "difference of opinion need not necessarily create ill feeling, differences as to facts can be settled one way or the other by reference to admitted authority. So that with courtesy in discussion it must be fair sailing."[7] *The Montana Post* issued a similar statement when it learned that the *Montana Democrat* soon would arrive in Virginia City. The *Post* vowed that its columns never would be used as a "partisan vehicle of blackguardism, personal abuse or scurrility of any kind" and counseled the *Democrat* to avoid petty political disputes and concentrate on advancing the material interests of Montana.[8]

That camp editors expected a war of words with their counterparts was largely the result of their understanding of American journalistic tradition. Most of them had been schooled according to the precepts of "personal journalism," a style of writing that prevailed in the majority of the nation's newspapers from the early 1830s until the outbreak of the Civil War. Prior to this era, newspapers were read primarily by a literate, intellectual elite and were valued for their erudite essays and political commentaries.[9] But the rise of the Penny Press changed all this. In the 1830s papers such as the *Boston Evening Herald*, the *New York Sun* and *The New York Herald* discovered the general public and abruptly altered the style and format of American journalism. Instead of learned literary articles, newspapers were filled with sensational stories choked with abusive, derisive language. Crimes of violence were reported in sordid detail; "enemies," especially rival editors, were attacked with relish and vengeance; and scandals involving society's most revered were given full, if not accurate, coverage. For their efforts, editors were rewarded with bulging subscription lists. The more vituperative their reporting, the more successful they became. During his investigative tour of the United States in 1831–32, Alexis De Tocqueville was astounded by the tone of the American press and was moved to remark that "the characteristics of the American journalist consist in an open and coarse appeal to the passions of his readers; he abandons principles to assail the characters of individuals, to track them into private life, and disclose all their weaknesses and vices. . . ."[10] The vastly expanded reading public expected and demanded sensationalism. Editors tumbled over themselves in their eagerness to break an important and particularly scandalous story and in the process developed fierce rivalries with their competitors. Indeed, open "press wars" became a daily feature of the penny newspapers. Editors saved their shrillest words for each other and had a fine time of it in detailing the gross "falsities" of their opponents. Subscribers, too, were enthralled by the combat and eagerly awaited each issue to see how their champion would respond to the enemy's latest charges.

Public enthusiasm for personal journalism, however, began to wane in the decade before the Civil War. Growing reader sophistication along with the rising tensions between North and South caused editors to devote more attention to legitimate news stories; little time was left for waging personal wars with rivals. Nonetheless, some editors rued the abandonment of personal journalism. As late as 1871, a veteran journalist for the *St. Louis Globe-Democrat* told a meeting of the Kansas Editors and Publishers' Association that American editors were never so powerful or exerted more influence over their readers than when they were "personal." To disavow personalities in journalism, he contended, would be to bankrupt the profession.[11]

Steeped in this tradition of personal journalism, camp editors were predisposed to expect a fight with their contemporaries. Further, the loose and easy environment of the frontier allowed them a freedom of expression largely unknown in the States. Thus, at a time when eastern newspapers were eschewing personalities, mining sheets continued and expanded the practice.

Editors who looked forward to a healthy fight with their "good looking cotemps" were not disappointed. From Montana and Wyoming to New Mexico and Arizona, camp newspapers engaged in frequent press wars equal to any that had occurred in the East. One amused western traveler observed that "of the two papers which exist in every [western] town, each is always at work attempting to 'use up' the other."[12] Bayard Taylor, another contemporary traveler, commented that the papers in Central City and Black Hawk, Colorado, seemed to be devoted full-time to attacking one another and that the "editorial dialect, to meet the tastes of the people is of an exceedingly free-and-easy character."[13] Thoroughly confounded by these mountain papers, Taylor could only describe them as "very curious specimens."[14] So accustomed was he to doing daily battle with his neighbors, one Montana editor felt compelled to report a lull in the festivities. "A kind of warlike peace prevails at present between us," he mused, "and as the [Deer Lodge] *Independent* takes strong political ground we think it would be but proper to have a diversion in that quarter before the next general engagement."[15] And a newspaper reader in Tuscon, Arizona, observed that when the editor of the *Arizona Citizen* entered into combat with his rival "editorial succeeded editorial, each more pungent and aggressive than its predecessor."[16]

For the camps' population, press battles provided amusing and entertaining reading, a pleasant diversion from the day's familiar drudgery. But for the editors, press wars held a far greater importance. They regarded them not simply as exercises in wit and insult performed for the benefit of eager readers; rather, they were serious affairs, the outcome of which often could influence the ultimate success or failure of a paper. Nevertheless, during the frontier era, camp journalists were ready at any time to engage in editorial combat with their contemporaries. In some instances they really had no choice, for the bases of conflict were real and readily apparent.

When two or more papers vied for the support of a common readership a bitter rivalry was almost certain to develop. Boom camps held great promise for journalists, but even in the most thriving mining district there was a limit to the number of papers that residents were financially able to sustain. The cost of living was high and what ready cash residents possessed usually was reserved for food and supplies. Further, many camp dwellers saw no point in subscribing to more than one local newssheet. These realities often were overlooked or ignored by would-be editors. Dazzled by the wealth of the mines and encouraged by the cosmopolitan nature of the mining frontier, they blithely established papers in camps that were already over-abundantly supplied. As a result, many of the papers were doomed to failure from the start. For example, by 1869 no less than three independently owned newspapers operated in Helena, Montana. *The Montana Post,* the territory's pioneer sheet and originally issued out of Virginia City, was the last to arrive. When business actvity began to slow in Virginia City, the *Post's* owners made the assumption that thriving Helena would welcome yet another paper in its midst. They were mistaken. After a year of financially ruinous competition with its two across-town rivals, the *Helena Herald* and the *Rocky Mountain Gazette,* the *Post* was forced into bankruptcy. Commenting on its demise the *Herald* pointed out: "The truth is . . . two daily newspapers can barely maintain themselves here. The third is the feather that breaks the camel's back. 'Let us have peace' and less newspapers until the growth, progress and importance of the Metropolis demand more."[17]

Veteran camp editors understood all this. When upstart contemporaries invaded what they considered their private domain, they interpreted the action as a direct and serious challenge to their own financial well-being. This peculiarity of camp journalists was noticed by John Bourke, an early resident of Tucson, Arizona, and a keen newspaper observer. In later years, Bourke recalled that the editor of Tucson's *Arizonan* reacted strongly to the arrival of the *Arizona Citizen.* "The establishment of the rival paper, the *Citizen,*" he explained, "was the signal for a war of words, waxing in bitterness from week to week, and ceasing only with the death of the *Arizonian* [sic] which took place not long after."[18] Editors not only unleashed an arsenal of vitriolic abuse against these new arrivals, but they also applied economic pressures to drive them from the field. To convince town residents that their paper was the superior product and one that deserved the support of all, they spared no expense to improve the appearance and quality of their paper. Overnight weeklies were converted into dailies; four column sheets were enlarged to six or eight; new and more elaborate type was purchased; "local" editors were hired to bring more diversity and depth to the personal columns; and job prices were reduced to encourage new advertising patronage.

A particularly expensive improvement was arranging to obtain the "latest" telegraphic dispatches from the East. In those communities where operating telegraph lines were only a distant hope, enterprising editors hired pony express riders to carry back the latest dispatches from the nearest completed station. Readers were delighted by this evidence of frontier ingenuity. After reading in his local paper news from the States that was only six days old, one very pleased Colorado miner wrote home to his family:

Only think of it for a moment. Receiving news thousands of miles, and for six hundred miles and over, on almost barren and uninhabited . . . region—having then printed and distributed all through the mountans in five days! That is doing things up with a rush, as every thing is done in the West.[19]

Editors who lacked the resources to purchase their own dispatches were equally enterprising. They patiently waited until their more wealthy competitor published the latest eastern intelligence and then unabashedly reprinted the items word for word in their own sheet. Those who could afford to buy the dispatches, of course, were incensed by the practice. *The Rocky Mountain News* accused its rival, the *Rocky Mountain Herald,* of "stealing" that which was rightly the property of the *News.*

We have never throughout the whole range of our editorial experience encountered a more contemptible and unscrupulous crew than those who now manage the . . .*Herald.* Utterly regardless of the truth, they concoct and publish the most scandalous falsehoods, distort facts, and with the impudence of highwaymen attempt to rob from others that which they have neither the industry nor the brains to procure otherwise.[20]

In Virginia City, *The Montana Post* scoffed at a rival sheet when it claimed to have made "special arrangements" with Western Union to obtain the latest news: "The only arrangements which have been made by the [*Rocky Mountain*] *Gazette* to obtain the 'late news' are evidently the following: To take from the columns of the *Post* all it requires and make its readers think they are getting the latest dispatches."[21] Papers charged with "stealing" from their neighbors, however, were quick to defend themselves. They argued that it was a waste of time and money for two newspapers to buy the same service and besides, once the telegrams appeared in print they became public property and were available to all.[22]

Their zeal to improve the quality of their paper often forced warring editors to take extreme measures to keep pace with the improvements of their competitors. When the *Rocky Mountain News* learned that its neighbor, the *Weekly Commonwealth,* had hired pony express riders to rush the latest editions of its paper to the mountain communities surrounding Denver, the *News* thought it necessary to organize its own pony express service. By 1863 both establishments claimed to have the faster riders, and both advertised that their paper reached mountain readers first. On one occasion, when the *Commonwealth* reached Central City a few minutes before the *News,* the latter accused its rival of violating the principles of fair play. According to the *News,* the *Commonwealth* "knowing its inability to compete with us fairly, yesterday omitted one and a half columns of important telegrams, in order to get off its pony ahead of us."[23] Mountain residents, of course, were delighted with the horse race, but for the *News* and the *Commonwealth* the "pony express war" was a financial sacrifice that neither could afford. Soon, both papers quietly discontinued the service and the mountain communities once again had to rely on their local sheets for the news.[24]

Editors also were concerned about the quality of their paper, and they spent much time and effort attempting to make it presentable and lively. They were especially proud of any original material they included and carefully examined the sheets of competitors to find any evidence of what they considered theft. *The Missoula Pioneer* was more than a little peeved when its larger and more prosperous neighbor, the *Helena Herald,* passed off as its own several important stories that had been lifted from the *Pioneer.* The paper was not about to let the "public wrong" go unanswered and hotly declared:

The right of mental property has never been questioned by honest men, and if . . . a valuable article finds its way into another journal, common courtesy binds the copyist to credit the source. . . . But there exists a class of newspaper-men who are obliged to cover their mental nakedness with garments woven by the brains of others.[25]

It was accepted practice to clip news items from exchanges, but to carry a story taken from another journal and claim it as original was considered a major breach of journalistic ethics. This point was made

clear by the editor of the Cimarron, New Mexico, *News and Press.*
Upon receiving the first issue of the *Las Vegas Eureka,* he noted that
his rival did not always give credit where credit was due and scolded:
"If you must steal, don't steal from your neighbor."[26] *The Rocky
Mountain Herald* was not amused when its two Denver contemporaries made a "habit" of stealing items from each other that originally
appeared in the *Herald:* "The *Daily News* copies from the *Weekly
Mountaineer,* news stolen from the *Herald,* and published more than
a week ago."[27]

Economic pressures were not the only causes for press wars. Political issues also divided the camp press and often were the source of
some of the most bitter exchanges. On the frontier where territorial
and local matters were taken seriously and hotly debated, it was
nearly impossible for papers to remain aloof from political discussions. Most papers eventually became outspoken advocates for a spe-
cific party or power group and fierce rivalries developed between
them. *The Weekly Arizona Miner* in Prescott told its readers that the
Tucson *Arizonan* was the organ of Richard C. McCormick, a candidate for Arizona's delegate to Congress, and was out to destroy the
Miner because it dared to support McCormick's opponent. In a strongly
worded editorial, the *Miner* exposed what it thought to be the *Arizonan*'s political purpose:

We had thought that the great Territory of Arizona was large enough for two
small newspapers, but it seems McCormick and his organ do not think so;
they want the *Miner* to die. . . . They want to reestablish the "dark age,"
when but one paper was published in the Territory, and that one paper was
owned and edited by his Excellency. . . .[28]

Even papers that espoused the same philosophy came into conflict.
Santa Fe's *Weekly Post* and the *New Mexican,* both Republican sheets,
argued over which of them was the "true voice" of the party. After the
New Mexican launched an attack charging the *Post* with "heretical
opinions," the *Post* shot back: "We cannot condescend to reply to so
ungentlemanly an assualt but we think it comes with very bad grace
from a Quantrell raider to talk about Republicanism."[29]

During and following the Civil War a favorite tactic used by camp
journalists to discredit rivals was to question their loyalty to the Union
cause. Democratic editors and those of Southern or foreign birth
were the most common targets of abuse, but not even the most loyal

Union man was safe from criticism. Rarely did an accuser make any effort to substantiate his charges. The fact that a rival was a Democrat or had never served in the Union army was proof enough of his "secessionist tendencies." Robert E. Fisk of the *Helena Herald* was outraged when James Mills, editor of the *Montana Post,* questioned his fidelity to the Union. In a long "explanation" he painstakingly detailed his "heroic" war record and even took major credit for organizing the first Republican national convention.[30] But for Mills, the *Herald* remained a "conceited hatchling scarcely yet out of the shell, and smelling badly from its rather peculiar incubation now comes up pompously and claims to be the worthy organ of the Union People of Montana. Bah!"[31] Seldom was the accused guilty of anything more than supporting a candidate or political position that was unacceptable to the opposition. Called a "disunion" paper by a Denver rival, the *Canon City Times* explained that "because the 'sapient editor' of the *Times* saw proper to stand upon their own political responsibility, and support 'their own pet' for Congress, that *reliable* sheet denounces us as secessionists and the publishers of a secession organ."[32]

Although politics provoked heated divisions, an especially embittered press war was likely between papers that spoke for rival mining settlements. Editors were tireless promoters of their camp and moved quickly to correct "false rumors" that could stampede onrushing gold-seekers to other communities. At the same time, they were only too willing to give credence to unfavorable reports they chanced to hear concerning the prospects of a rival district. *The Arizona Citizen* in Tucson took exception to an article in the Santa Fe *New Mexican* giving credence to the remarks of a former and much disgruntled Arizona miner. According to the *Citizen:*

The *New Mexican* exhibits a trait in its item entirely too common with the journalistic fraternity. Failing to note some local evidence of prosperity, the record of which would do the place credit, ye local journalist too often keeps an eye out for a discontented mortal who has recently abandoned some other locality and just arrived in his, and easily finding one, the usual item, such as we quote from the *New Mexican,* follows with such bombastic comment as eminently befits that style of journalism.[33]

The Rocky Mountain News was similarly provoked by the efforts of the *Moreno Lantern* in Elizabethtown, New Mexico, to cast doubt upon the future of the Colorado mines. Warning the *Lantern* to stop its "rumor mongering tactics," the *News* speculated that the editor of the *Lantern* "seems to have started out with the idea that the proper way to build up his own locality is to decry and depreciate Colorado."[34]

Most editors were more vehement in the defense of their camp. *The Sweetwater Mines* in South Pass City, Wyoming, was beside itself when the *Helena Herald* suggested that the mines on the Sweetwater River were less than productive and might be nothing more than a cruel hoax perpetrated by greedy promoters. Declaring that the "puny efforts of a thousand such slanderous sheets as the *Herald* can no more retard our progress and development than can the Niagara be dammed with straw,"[35] the *Mines* angrily predicted that the "conglomerate mass of filth and corruption" running the *Herald* office would no doubt find its proper reward in a "narrow apartment of the 'hell-box'."[36] Instead of matching insult for insult, the *Herald* contemptuously refused to acknowledge the *Mines'* existence and continued to warn prospectors away from the South Pass region. After all, neither the struggling *Mines* nor the Sweetwater diggings posed much of a threat to Helena's future development. But a report originating from its arch rival, Virginia City's *Montana Post,* produced a far different effect. According to the *Post,* the mines of the Coeur d'Alene mountains in Idaho were of exceptional quality and it urged all Montanans, especially the miners of Helena, to personally investigate them. The *Herald* saw this as an attempt by its rival to reestablish Virginia City as a major commercial and supply center and to draw population away from Helena. Charging "conspiracy," the paper asked all who were loyal to Montana to actively work to drive the *Post* from the territory;

We here charge that those who lend countenance and aid to the unscrupulous *Montana Post,* are bolstering up an enemy to the Territory; they are nourishing a viper that has turned and stung them, and will do it again on the first occasion; they are giving support to a set of men . . . who will scruple at nothing that is vile and treacherous in the persecution of their base ends. . . .[37]

Not all press wars were fought over substantive issues. Conditioned to see "personality" lurking behind every criticism or stray remark, camp editors were quick to charge their rivals with "ungentlemanly conduct" and to take offense at real or imagined slights. Thus, some disputes arose simply because editors had an intense personal dislike for one another. Such was the case, as mentioned in chapter 2, between two Denver editors, William Byers and Thomas Gibson. Partners in the spring of 1859 when the *Rocky Mountain News* was founded, the two never felt comfortable with each other, and soon parted company. By 1860 each ran a newspaper in Denver, and the bad feeling between them now was given full expression in their newspapers. Gibson alternately referred to his former partner as a "fool," "knave," and "liar," while to Byers, Gibson was a common criminal guilty of land fraud, a Britisher with a pronounced Cockney accent, and he even went so far as to print a drawing of the rear view of an ass, with the caption: "A life-like portrait of the sensitive editor of the *Herald*. Copyright secured."[38] And so it went. For the next several years the two editors flailed at one another, neither able to abide the other. Finally, in January of 1864, Gibson was forced to admit defeat. Wearied and financially battered by the long battle, he sold his paper and moved out of the territory.[39]

While engaged in these very personal disputes, camp editors eagerly sought out the character flaws of their enemies, and they were not hesitant to use what they found. Those who frequented town saloons or gambling halls or who were known to enjoy a drink were especially vulnerable to character assassination in the press. Revealed by a rival as a former bartender in a "sleazy" drinking establishment, James Mills of the Deer Lodge *New North-West* admitted that "there is more truth than poetry in the charge," but reminded readers that "when the *Helena Herald* was waging its high-toned crusade against the *Montana Post*, the Editor of the *Herald* was gathered up, drunk, in the gutters of Helena and hauled home repeatedly [while, at the same time] its 'sub' editor was tied in bed, drunk. . . ."[40] So frequently was Ovando J. Hollister of the Black Hawk, Colorado, *Daily Mining Journal* called an "unhappy drunk" by his contemporaries that his "junior" thought it necessary to come to his defense. Under a column entitled "Very Personal," the "junior" agreed that his "senior" made no pretentions to total abstinence, but "we believe he doesn't therefore care to be always introduced to the Denver people as a 'drunkard,' a 'misanthrope,' or an 'infidel'. . . ."[41] These attacks abated somewhat when Hollister left the *Journal* and began a history of the Colorado goldrush. His return to jouranlism as the managing editor of the *Daily Rocky Mountain News*, however, brought renewed attacks. This time when referring to his "excessive" drinking habits, his enemies mentioned him by name or by initials, a practice the beleaguered Hollister thought particularly reprehensible. "What word," he cried, "shall adequately characterize the rudeness of one who not only addresses a cotemporary . . . by his name or initials, but prints those initials in 'lower case?' It is on a par with spitting in one's face."[42] His objections had little effect. Not until he quit Colorado journalism to take up a real estate business in Utah did his peers of the press treat him with dignity and respect.[43] Perhaps this aggressive trait of frontier journalists was best described by a contemporary Wyoming observer when he remarked that one "old-time" Wyoming editor could "sling more mud with a teaspoon" than "modern" editors could "with a scoopshovel."[44]

Whatever their causes, camp press wars followed a fairly predictable pattern. Established papers usually greeted new arrivals with guarded expressions of welcome and good will. Newcomers were praised for their enterprise and their sheets were described as "lively" or "well-filled" and calculated to advance the best interests of the territory. *The Laramie Daily Sentinel* was greeted so cordially by its contemporaries that its editor expressed concern that he might become "egotistic."[45] Much of this good feeling was genuine. Editors who had founded their own papers were well aware of the time and effort it took to operate a frontier sheet and they could sympathize with their new competitor. As one New Mexico editor put it: "We know that an editor has to stand knocks and cuffs from all sides with but few thanks from anybody, for we have 'been there'."[46] Not all new arrivals, of course, were received with open arms. *The Weekly Arizona Miner* in Prescott noted the appearance of the Elizabethtown, New Mexico, *Press and Telegraph* by declaring that it was not the ablest or best printed newspaper in the territories, but allowed that "its conductors do the best they can with the means at their disposal."[47] Central City's *Daily Miners' Register* (Colorado) was less kind when it reviewed the first issue of the *Boulder County News*. "Without an exception," it growled, "it is the most miserably printed sheet we ever saw." The *Register* went on to say that since the *News* possessed no "redeeming characteristics" whatsoever it was a "disgrace" to Colorado and should not be supported.[48] But for the most part, editors avoided criticism of newly founded sheets and kept whatever misgivings they had to themselves.[49]

When attention was drawn to a rival's grammatical or typographical errors or to his "confused" thinking on various issues, it usually was a sign that the "Era of Good Feelings" was drawing to a close and a full-blown press war was imminent. Still, at this stage in the conflict, editors couched their attacks in the form of gentle "reminders;" rivals were chided for their "orthographical" blunders, for their failure to properly identify stories "lifted" from exchanges, for not clearly defining their position on important politcal issues, and for allowing "dead" advertising to pad their columns. Soon, the "reminders" gave way to more pointed advice, which in turn provoked more heated replies. In Virginia City, the *Montana Democrat* expressed "surprise" over the change in editors of the *Montana Post* and wondered aloud whether there might be some "sinister" purpose behind the move. The *Post* testily replied that "we respectfully decline the controversy you are evidently seeking. We can devote our columns to a better purpose, and are content to see your paper and that of your Helena antagonist devoted to personal attacks and recriminations. Please consider us out; and, if it is not asking too much of a favor, permit the *Post* to do as it pleases."[50] Yet for some papers it was impossible to do as they pleased. Fearing that any criticism might damage their standing in the community and seriously threaten their chances for survival, editors felt it necessary to refute every charge, every innuendo, to defend themselves against every sarcasm—and do it in the strongest possible terms.[51]

The white heat of a press war was characterized by a fury and intensity that allowed no room for retreat or surrender. While this stage lasted, editors threw all caution to the wind and used any argument, any piece of information or bit of gossip to convince readers that their opponents were unfit to publish a paper and were a disgrace to the good name of the territory. At a time and in a place where the laws governing libel were ill-defined and almost impossible to enforce, it was common for warring editors to accuse each other of the most heinous and bizarre crimes. A press war in Tucson between the *Daily Arizona Citizen* and the *Arizona Weekly Star* was representative of many. After L. C. Hughes of the *Star* branded R. C. Brown's *Citizen* an obscene organ filled with malicious slander, Brown directly assailed Hughes' character. Calling his rival a thief, liar, and coward, a "Pin-Head" accustomed to using "female and young as foil," Brown added the charge of adultery to Hughes' supposed crimes: "It might be well to remind the public that this sensitive and high-souled scoundrel is the same man . . . to have boastingly confessed to adultery with the wife of an absent friend. . . ."[52] In Helena a similar battle raged, with the editor of the *Helena Herald* openly declaring his considered opinion that his counterpart of the *Rocky Mountain Gazette* deserved the less than friendly attention of town toughs.

Scornfully referring to the *Gazette* as the "Mezeppa" he warned the "Mezeppa-man" that unless he drastically altered the course of his paper an outraged populace would no doubt invade his office and with tar and feathers offer him a free ride on a rail. "So have a care, thou foul-mouthed slanderer," said the *Herald* in a parting shot, "the evils you would have visited on others may full soon overtake thyself."[53]

Violent encounters often resulted from such intemperate outbursts. In Denver, Frederick J. Stanton, the always angry editor of the *Daily Gazette,* had occasion to display his fighting talents during a dispute with William N. Byers, editor of the *Rocky Mountain News.* Throughout the summer of 1865, Stanton hammered away at Byers charging him with using his position as Postmaster of Denver to delay and even destroy important documents belonging to the *Gazette.* The more Byers denied the allegations, the more insistent Stanton became. Finally, Stanton announced that the matter was now "personal" and unless the missing documents were produced he would teach Byers a "lesson" he would never forget. To this threat Byers replied with biting sarcasm:

Ye great historian threatens to break that new cane . . . over our tow head, but whenever you feel an irresistible desire to break a cane over our tow head . . . summon all your self-denial, for our schooling for the past three or four years has not taught us much respect for cowardly Copperheads. That is all.[54]

Stanton made one last effort to obtain the "missing documents" through persuasion in the press. This time Byers took the offensive: he charged that there were "many" in Denver who were of the opinion that Stanton's children, under the guidance of an "older head," were the thieves who "took the letters."[55] Stanton was incensed. In a rage he sought Byers out and armed with a stout hickory stick brutally caned his surprised rival repeatedly across the head. The next morning the *News* likened the assault to that made by John Wilkes Booth on Abraham Lincoln:

The spirit that animated the cowardly brute who made his dastardly attack is the same that animated John Wilkes Booth in his attack that made desolate the hearts of the American people, only that the would-be assassin . . . lacks the courage of his teacher (Booth) in Copperheadism.[56]

Although knocked unconscious by the blows and unable to defend himself because of an old shoulder wound suffered during a street fight in Omaha,[57] Byers was not seriously injured and quickly recovered. For his part in the affray, Stanton lost the advertising patronage of more than eighty-five Denver merchants and, as a result, soon was forced to suspend operations.[58]

Press wars that reached this level of intensity had to be somehow resolved. Few camps, however bright their future, could condone behavior that might bring notoriety to the region or create an unfavorable impression abroad. Battling editors understood this. Thus, most press wars either concluded by a mutual agreement among the combatants to "prevent the infliction of personalities on the public, and secure good will among the members of the profession"[59] or by the abrupt and forced withdrawal of one of the principals. And when the war was over, all concerned could breathe easier knowing that there were other and far greater issues to be discussed and resolved.

5

"Forbearance
Ceases to Be
a Virtue"

By the late 1850s most Americans believed that they had some notion of what life was like in a distant boom camp. Goldseekers who returned home from the Mother Lode Country of California carried with them rousing stories of the lawlessness of mining communities, of bands of desperadoes hunted down by vigilante committees, of quick-fingered monte and faro dealers who swaggered through the town's casinos and saloons, and of kind-hearted ladies who were always ready to work their charms on any down-on-his-luck prospector. The nation's newspapers also helped spread these colorful and often exaggerated tales, and soon the day of the Forty-niners entered American folk history and legend.[1] Later, when mining excitements stampeded thousands of fortune hunters into the Rocky Mountains, many who ventured West were ill-prepared for the realities of camp living. Much of what they had heard and read of life in the California and Rocky Mountain mines had little resemblance to what they encountered in such camps as Black Hawk, Colorado; Tombstone, Arizona; or Silver City, New Mexico. Panning and cradling for gold, they discovered, was long, backbreaking work; gambling halls, far from palatial, were more often dirt-floored tents and cabins; and the hurdy-gurdy girls who were in evidence were a far cry from the dark-eyed beauties of newspaper accounts.

Nor was there anything romantic about camp lawlessness. As in the earlier diggings of California, incidents of crime, vice, and violence occurred in many fledgling communities in the Rocky Mountain mining frontier and were of deep concern to law-abiding residents and civic leaders. For example, in Bannack and Virginia City, Montana, an organized gang of highwaymen preyed on the traffic moving along the roads and brought a reign of terror to the scattered mining settlements. Between the summer of 1862 and the fall of 1863 this outlaw band, led by Henry Plummer, seriously disrupted the mails and gold shipments and was responsible for the murders of over one hundred people.[2] Violent crime was equally troublesome in Denver City during the first two years of its existence. Brawls and shooting affrays were common in the town's many drinking and gambling halls, prompting one outraged observer to remark that "there is no law, no jails, no penitentiaries, & no courts in this country; the consequence is that there is no restraint on human passion."[3] In Cimarron, New Mexico, lawlessness even entered the courtroom. During the course of a murder trial, the *Cimarron News* was appalled by the behavior of the court's onlookers:

We have no power here to enforce the disarming of spectators, but it is very unseemly to have the justice room filled with partisans of either side armed to the teeth. It is entirely subversive of our old fashioned notions of the solemnity of justice, too, to have the whole court, prisoner and all—save and except the judge—adjourn, in the midst of a trial for life and death, to have a drink. This reads grotesque to those at a distance, but is not so to those who dwell here.[4]

It was during these initial hell-days that many western editors made their appearance in the camps and founded their newspapers. Like other arriving immigrants, journalists too were often surprised and overwhelmed by the rampant crime they encountered. But violence presented a special problem to the men of print. On one hand, their self-appointed role was to promote the camp and to convince distant readers of its boundless future; yet, they also had a time-cherished responsibility to speak out against crime and injustice. With a sizable investment in the future of the town, these camp editors then found themselves in an uncomfortable position—whether to report accurately and to combat forcefully the lawlessness that they witnessed or to ignore it. In the beginning most chose the easier course and simply ignored it. They did this in part because they had an abiding faith in the land, and because they were as yet unfamiliar with their surroundings. Virginia City's *Montana Post* indicated its confusion over the proper course to pursue when it assured readers that there was a marked improvement in the moral tone of the young camp's society and "law now reigns supreme."[5] Yet in the same issue, partially obscured in the "local items," the paper matter-of-factly reported one suicide, one stabbing, and one case of animal cruelty where some town rowdy intentionally half-butchered and partially paralyzed a hog and then allowed the crazed animal to drag itself along the camp's main business street.[6]

Many editors feared that by reporting acts of violence they would frighten off decent families from immigrating and discourage much needed eastern capital. Thus, the Silver City, New Mexico *Tribune* announced its intention to omit from its columns "needless" details of common street brawls since townsfolk were well informed of them anyway. Besides, the paper argued, eastern readers might "misunderstand" such items.[7] Nearly a decade later, the *Tombstone Epitaph* echoed the same sentiment when it criticized its across-town competitor, the *Nugget*, for reviewing in detail the "bygone" events leading to the famed shootout at the OK Corral between the "Cowboys" and the Earp brothers. Such ill-timed sensationalism, said the *Epitaph*, could only retard the economic growth of the city.[8]

To convince outside readers of the camp's peaceful intent, editors often alluded to the number of families who dwelled safely within the community. *The Daily Miners' Register* in Central City, Colorado, begrudgingly admitted to the presence of a rough and ready element in the camp, but quickly added: "We have a large number of families here, and the number is constantly increasing and will increase." The paper continued by predicting that in a few months time, Central City's "society" would be "not one whit behind any other city in a State or Territory."[9] In a similar vein, *The Pueblo Chieftain* acknowledged that Pueblo had acquired some notoriety for its free and easy moral tone but at least "no one need ever lock his door here for fear of robbery," and pointed to the increasing number of families who were making the town their home.[10] Perhaps overstating the case, one Wyoming editor denied altogether the existence of any criminal element in his community: "Our city is favored above all the world in its quiet and good order, the absence of crimes, rows and accidents, no devastating fires, and a good and peaceful state of affairs."[11]

Despite this original reluctance to publicly discuss incidents of camp lawlessness, when frequent brawls, shootings, and thefts went unchallenged by legally constituted authorities, western journalists moved swiftly to help restore law and order. Lawbreakers were told in no uncertain terms that unless they mended their nefarious ways, they would gain the full attention of the camp's newspaper. The *Daily*

Miner's Register of Central City, Colorado, warned a band of toughs who persisted in making wild rides through the camp's crowded streets that "we will publish the names of such persons. . . . They want notoriety and we propose to assist them to it."[12] The holdup of a long-awaited mail and express wagon spurred the outraged *Cimarron News* to call for prompt retaliatory action and charged that "such men as Taylor and his companions will not only commit robbery, but ere long we may . . . hear of murder and other outrages being committed."[13] The *Prescott Weekly Arizona Miner* also made known its intention to print the names of those persons who disturbed the public peace. After editorially scolding one "Mr. Dennis" for frequenting town saloons and letting whiskey get the better of him, the *Miner* gave the man this advice:

Now Dennis, when liquor has not had the best of him has . . . acted as a good citizen should act; but, as this is his third or fourth bad performance, we hope the punishment he has received and the sense of shame it must bring upon him, will, in future, cause him to let intoxicating liquors alone, and abandon rowdyism.[14]

Public officials and law officers also received their share of editorial attention. One concern of camp editors was the condition of the town's jail. Fearful that dangerous criminals might easily break out of the flimsy structures that variously passed as jails, the press called upon mayors and city council members to perform their civic duty and provide the camp with an "escape-proof" facility.[15] These entreaties were not always answered. In Denver, editor William Byers of the *Rocky Mountain News* bombarded municipal leaders with demands for a new and secure jailhouse, but to no avail. Finally, the public-minded editor donated to the money-conscious council a suitable building for the purpose.[16] Sheriffs, too, were reminded of their duty. Tucson's *Weekly Star* provided the details of a shootout in which a prominent townsman was killed and then strongly attacked the sheriff and his deputies for allowing the crime to go unchallenged: "Are our authorities to let such crimes pass unnoticed, that the murderers can continue to prey upon settlers whenever their blood stained hands itch to take the life of a fellow man."[17] Nor did judges escape caustic criticism. The *Canon City Times* let known its considerable displeasure when a local judge assessed only a "paltry" five dollar fine against a man who had stabbed and killed his neighbor during a quarrel.[18] And Wyoming's *South Pass News* demanded a "full and adequate administration of the civil and penal laws of the land" to head off an aroused citizenry from engaging in extralegal vigilante acts.[19]

In every young mining community gambling and drinking halls and "hurdy-gurdy" houses flourished and were often the first businesses that newcomers encountered. One Tombstone editor boasted about the great numbers of gamblers in his community noting:

It is generally believed that the prosperity of a mining town may be estimated by the amount of gambling going on. If this be the case, we are certainly on the high road to prosperity, as the gambling tables are nightly crowded. . . .[20]

The editor of Virginia City's *Montana Post* also viewed the existence of the camp's many gambling and dancing establishments with some amusement. After calling attention to the "huge" crowds that gathered nightly in the various hurdy-gurdy houses, he observed that the young men in attendance seemed to thoroughly enjoy themselves.[21]

These public expressions of approval, however, were the exception rather than the rule. While the editors seemed to accept the necessity of amusement centers and even were known to patronize them on occasion, they refrained from according them more than passing notice in their columns. But when they became the scenes of frequent rows and as public drunkenness noticeably increased, editors abandoned their former silence and vigorously campaigned against camp vice. For example, the building of a "keno house" next door to the camp's concert hall provoked the *Daily Miners' Register* in Central City, Colorado, to break its former silence and urge the closing of all such businesses since there was a city ordinance banning them.[22] *The Boulder County Pioneer* went further in its efforts against vice and unrelentingly attacked the community's liquor dealers and saloonkeepers. The paper piously advised those who trafficked in liquor to find another and less demeaning line of work:

We can only wish for them what we have often heard them wish for themselves, that they could find some decent business . . . , a business in which they might hold up their heads, and not wear a perpetual blush in the sight of moral, upright humanity.[23]

Public drunkenness became such a nuisance in Silver City, New Mexico, that the editor of the camp's paper called for all "god-fearing" women of the community to organize a Temperance Lodge to aid in restoring sobriety and reality to the many men who were held captive by "demon rum."[24]

Town brothels were another major target of editorial wrath. So-called sporting houses arrived in the camp almost as early as gambling and drinking halls, but again editors initially hesitated to speak out against their existence. As long as prostitutes confined themselves to the backstreets and were discreet in plying their trade, most editors were content to leave them alone. *The Weekly Colorado Miner* in Georgetown explained its silence this way: "We do not know that it is anymore the duty of a journalist to undertake to mend the morals and manners of a commmunity. This we do know that the social evil which is said to exist in our midst, is not catching, if let alone."[25] The Deer Lodge, Montana, *New North-West* was of a similar mind. "Certain parties," the paper reported, had broken the windows of a Chinese "crib," and the girls had answered the attack with gunfire. Pointing out that this particular brothel was located on a main street in clear view of honest citizens, the paper declared that Chinese prostitutes "have more brazen effrontery than the native-borns, who take to retired streets." *The New North-West* thought this noxious and urged legislation that would confine these establishments to less visible areas of town.[26]

However, when sporting houses began to pose a serious threat to the public peace and safety, journalists called upon authorities to either control the wanton lawlessness that occurred in them or to close them down altogether. In Denver City, the *Weekly Rocky Mountain News* expressed its concern over a rash of fires recently set in the city's notorious "riverfront district." The paper agreed that the fires, no doubt set by well-meaning citizens, caused an abatement of the social evil, but it warned that the flames easily could spread to other parts of the camp and thus endanger the lives of all residents. "Will either the civil or the military authorities," pleaded the *News*, "take prompt and efficient steps to avert the danger and protect the lives and property of our citizens?"[27] On the other side of town, the *Weekly Commonwealth* also reported on the activities of the arsonists and expressed the opinion that while public brothels might be a "necessity" in a camp as raw as Denver, they must be controlled and held in a "wholesome check, so that public decency should not be outraged." Using curious logic, the paper went on to opine: "Dancing and drinking must be stopped in such houses, or the community is not safe from the danger which any night may happen to it."[28] *The Laramie Daily Sentinel* was particularly exercised when a brothel suddenly appeared directly across the street from its office. Abandoning its former silence on the subject, the *Sentinel* launched an intensive investigation into the disturbances caused by houses of ill-repute; when one "Maggie Wallace" testified in open court about her trade, the paper provided full details, including the names of some of her more prominent patrons.[29]

Campaigns against lawlessness were not restricted to the camp and its immediate environs. Related to and at times overshadowing camp violence were Indian depredations occurring in the mountains and along the roads leading to mining settlements. Editors reacted strongly to any reports of Indian attacks, and most journals were insistent in their demands for the government to follow a strict policy of extermination toward the tribes. The editor of Central City's *Daily Miners' Register* admitted that some eastern do-gooders might charge him with "inhumanity and all that sort of bosh," but he nevertheless voiced his conviction that the military should offer a fifty dollar bounty for the scalps of *"men, women and children."* However, if this should look unduly brutal in the statute books, he suggested the law be amended to read "'a reward of fifty dollars for Indian scalps,' thus including all ages and sizes."[30]

To almost all western journalists, the Indian was subhuman, a savage incapable of learning the ways of civilized man. According to the *Sweetwater Mines* of South Pass City, Wyoming:

Cruelty manifests itself in the first traits of character developed in the pappoose [sic]. He delights in torturing little animals that may fall into his hands. He is not educated to do so, but inherently he takes pleasure in causing pain, and revels with delight amid the demonstrations of it.[31]

Far from the picturesque "Noble Savage" of eastern fictionalists and humanitarians, camp editors believed the Indian to be a "brute, a vermin-swarming, lazy, treacherous savage, that comes like the wind, and leaves but a mass of smoldering ruins, and mutilated bodies, where yesterday was a happy home."[32] The Golden City, Colorado, *Transcript* perhaps spoke for most western journals when it declared:

It were better that every Indian were killed by the bullet, and his bones thrown to the wolves . . . than that one man or one fair Saxon woman should ever cower in fright . . . at the hands of these red fiends who now seek to recover by barbaric war, the possession of that which destiny long since took from them for a nobler use.[33]

Editors also reserved some of their harshest criticism for their military protectors. The presence of soldiers was usually welcomed in the West; during Indian troubles, military and civilian authorities were besieged by demands for protection. But the arrival of soldiers was often a mixed blessing. Uncle Sam's troops often had little resemblance to the chivalrous warriors of romantic literature. Instead of disciplined protectors of the peace, often they were ill-trained, ill-clothed, ill-fed and, in some instances, ill-mannered. Further, when "liquored up" by a generous bartender, the men in blue were likely to contribute to the camp's lawlessness, a fact that did not escape attention in the press. Denver's *Colorado Republican,* after witnessing the behavior of nearby stationed soldiers, hotly observed:

Talk about Indians, they are princes with all their dirty, filthy habits to a rank of soldiers loafing about a city. Troops are all right in their place, but they have no business to be stationed where they will be in the way of communities. . . .[34]

In a continuing effort to control military rowdiness, the paper beseeched Denver's saloon owners and liquor dealers to refuse whiskey to any trooper and demanded local authorities to punish "those scoundrels who sell to soldiers that which begets crime."[35]

These untempered demands for a return to law and order, for an end to vice and violence, did not go unchallenged by the camps' lawless element; indeed they often provoked an immediate and violent response. William Byers, editor of Denver's *Rocky Mountain News* was so frequently the target of abuse for his strong stand against crime that his office took on the appearance of an armed camp. During the summer of 1860, Byers directed much of his editorial efforts against Charles Harrison, the gun-slinging owner of the Criterion Saloon, the town's most notorious and dangerous gambling and drinking emporium. When Harrison added yet another to his long list of victims, Byers unleashed a heated editorial attack against the gambler and called upon all honest citizens to help bring the man to justice. Even before copies of the *News* reached the streets, members of Harrison's gang invaded the editor's office, yanked him out of his chair and half-dragged and shoved him over to the Criterion. Here they prepared to hang him from a beam over the bar but Harrison, apparently fearing the consequences of such a rash act, quickly slipped the thoroughly shaken editor out a back door. Byers ran back to his office, armed himself and his small staff of assistants, and when his kidnappers reappeared, this time they were met by a blast of rifle and shotgun fire. In the shootout, one of the gang was killed and two others captured. Later, a "People's Court" banished the arrested men from Denver, but Harrison was absolved of any guilt in the affair.[36]

Byers was not the only newspaperman in Denver to experience the violence of the camp at first hand. Thomas Gibson of the *Rocky Mountain Herald* also became a target of town ruffians. After Gibson had chided nearby stationed soldiers for their "drunken revelries" and made unfavorable comparisons between their behavior and that of "wild Indians," a squad of troopers broke into the *Herald* office, shot and critically wounded one of the printers and, after destroying several presses, rode off unmolested into the night.[37] In Cimarron, New Mexico, the *News and Press* suffered an even worse fate. Angered by the paper's editorial policies on a number of topics, a mob seized the office, drove out the editor and effectively silenced the paper by the skillful use of a large charge of well-placed black powder.[38]

Despite the threats and actual attacks made against them, most editors continued their struggle against crime and vice. When Andrew J. Fisk of the *Helena Daily Herald* was "called out" by a hired gunman because of his articles exposing the illegal practices of a "sugar ring" in Helena, Fisk, no stranger to a gun, easily got the "drop" on his assailant but he told readers that "the day has long gone . . . in Montana when disputes . . . are to be settled upon the streets with six-shooters; and the freedom of the American press is as much an established fact as the Constitution, and it cannot be trammelled nor bullied by a man or set of men."[39] Similarly, Hezekiah S. Johnson, editor of the *Santa Fe Weekly Gazette,* informed his public that his enemies had tried to silence him by setting fire to his office. But he boldly declared that the "insignificant libels on manhood thought they could stop the wheel of progress by kindling a little fire in the corner of one room of a printing office! What ignorance!"[40] In response to "advice" from Denver's large gambling crowd to cease his activities against them, Simon Whiteley of the *Daily Commonwealth* vowed to continue his efforts and announced in a "public card" that the "advice which has been tendered to the editor of this paper by friends of the gamblers is thrown away. Nobody is going to assault him by day or night."[41]

Exhortations in the press against lawlessness, however, were not

always met with success. In those mining districts where legally constituted law enforcement agencies were either ineffective or nonexistent, editors encouraged the law-abiding population to use extralegal
means of quieting chronic lawbreakers and violators of the public
peace. This extreme step was not taken without some trepidation. To
admit that violence and crime had gotten out of hand was a poor way
to induce immigration or attract eastern capital. But under certain
circumstances many editors felt they had no choice. As Thomas Dimsdale, the pioneer editor of Virginia City's *Montana Post,* explained:
"Where justice is powerless as well as blind, the strong arm of the
mountaineer must wield her sword; for 'self-preservation is the first
law of nature'."[42] William Byers of the *Rocky Mountain News* put it
another way. Reporting that a gang of horse thieves had run off with
some sixteen horses and mules in the "last three days," he declared
that "forbearance ceases to be a virtue" and called upon the population to adopt "desperate measures" to establish law and order. What
the outraged editor had in mind was a resort to vigilante justice and
the quick law of "Judge Lynch." "We give these rascals warning," he
said, "that if they are caught they will be called upon to dance upon
nothing—and caught they will be."[43] Two weeks later Byers returned
to his theme of "forbearance ceases to be a virtue" and detailed the
arrest and punishment of one James Hanna. Suspected of being a
member of the gang that was causing so much havoc in and around
Denver, Hanna was offered "leniency" by a vigilante committee if he
would disclose the whereabouts of his compatriots. Hanna readily
agreed to the proposition, but after a few hours of futile riding on the
plains east of Denver, the out-of-patience vigilantes pulled up at a
convenient cottonwood tree where they "hung" the hapless horse
thief "for a short time," and then administered fifty lashes to his back.
Finally they tied him to his horse, pointed him in the general direction of Kansas and sent him on his way. Of this example of vigilante
justice, Byers wrote: "We hope this will be a warning to all who may
feel disposed to take horses without leave, for depend upon it, the
next one caught will not be dealt with so leniently."[44]

In Hanna's case, the vigilantes at least applied their punishment
with a certain degree of legality. A People's Court consisting of a
president, clerk and twelve jurymen examined the evidence against
Hanna and only after extended debate did it go about its self-appointed
duty.[45] But in some instances, editors showed a preference for "Judge
Lynch." In Black Hawk, Colorado, the *Daily Mining Journal* observed

that incidents of rape and attempted rape were on the increase in the camp and reported that a young Negro babysitter had been attacked the night before. "Certain parties," the paper averred, knew the identify of the intruder and wondered aloud: "Why he was not secured and dosed with a preparation of Lynch Law, we are unable to see."[46] *The Laramie Daily Sentinel* also expressed a willingness to wink at lynch law. It denounced those residents who "go about the country a walking arsenal," and warned that if these men did not disarm themselves immediately, "we will advoate a return to lynch law as a means of self-protection."[47]

Still, editors were anxious to see an end to extralegal justice and were quick to disavow any unnecessary action taken by vigilante groups. When the *Sweetwater Mines* heard rumblings that a vigilante committee was organizing in South Pass City, the *Mines* hotly proclaimed that the camp was well protected by its police force and that should the group engage in any extralegal activity then it would be hunted down until all its members were properly punished.[48] A midnight lynching in Deer Lodge, Montana, also was severely condemned by the camp newspaper. *The New North-West* reminded its readers that every illegal hanging was an advertisement to the outside world that a state of anarchy existed in Montana and thus retarded the growth and development of the territory. The day was long past, it continued, when such actions were necessary and

the death of that Chinaman, guilty or guiltless, dragged beyond the temple of justice without a hearing, and slain like a dog, is a disgrace and a crime. Chinaman, alien, pagan, depraved as he may have been, his blood-clots stain deep on the record of Montana. We trust the Pine tree will bear no more such fruit.[49]

By urging public authorities to attend vigorously to their duties, by calling for the swift prosecution of lawbreakers, by campaigning against vice and corruption, by boldly publishing the names of known criminals and, when all else failed, by advocating the organization of vigilante groups, the camp press was a powerful voice in the community for law and order and an effective weapon against rampant lawlessness. Although this period of unrest was usually short-lived, while it lasted it monopolized the crusading efforts of many editors. Only when these initial days of crime and violence were spent could they direct their full attention to the more positive causes that also were of vital importance to the welfare and future of the community.

6

Crusaders
for
Permanency

Little about the appearance of most Rocky Mountain mining camps excited the civic pride of their founders. Crowded into narrow gulches or sprawled across barren hillsides, the camps could boast of a few rough-hewn log cabins, but for the most part only temporary shelters and loosely constructed wood-frame buildings greeted newcomers. While hotels and boarding houses were in evidence, they too were hastily erected and offered visitors little more than a space for sleeping. The camps' streets also contributed to the dreary appearance of the towns. The main thoroughfare, along which stood the various supply stores, saloons, and businesses, was deeply rutted and, depending on the weather and the time of year, either choked with dust or ankle-deep in mud. A further indication of the crudeness of these early mining centers was the noticeable absence of churches and schools, of libraries and reading rooms, and other harbingers of permanency and civilization.

That the camps lacked familiar comforts and institutions, however, was of little importance to most goldseekers. Their aim was not so much to create a new home in the mountain West as it was to find quick and easy wealth. To them the camp was only a diversion from the serious business of working nearby streambeds and tearing from the land its illusive flecks of gold and other precious minerals. In any case, most miners had no intention of making the camps their permanent residence. On the contrary, many considered themselves only as visitors and eagerly awaited the day when they could return to their homes in the States.

Established under the most frantic and chaotic of circumstances, situated in the most unlikely of places, the camps grew almost by themselves, without direction and without purposeful planning. Thus, they were communities only in the sense that they were centers of population, for they lacked that spirit of unity and purpose which characterized older and more normally founded villages and towns. Moreover, many of the camps initially operated without formal and legal institutions of government. Police and fire protection, town rules and regulations, and mining laws often were controlled by the body politic in mass meetings, or by fiat of self-constituted People's Courts. This unstructured state of society was tolerable to transients and stampeders, but for those who had a sizable investment not in the mines but in the community itself, it was essential that life and purpose somehow be infused into the camp and that it develop a feeling and identity of its own.

Among those most interested in the permanency of the community were frontier editors. Like shopkeepers, supply dealers, and other businessmen, their livelihood depended upon the vitality of the camp and its promise for future development. Accordingly, they immediately set about the task of not only promoting the region and inducing immigration and eastern capitol, but they also deeply involved themselves in the internal activities of their chosen community. There was much for them to do. Unlike their eastern counterparts who worked in a stable environment where laws and familiar institutions were of long standing and taken as a matter of course, early western journalists directed their editorial energies toward introducing the trappings of culture and civilization.

But before they could begin this great task, newly established editors often found themselves preoccupied with the role of the camp booster. Mining camps were highly volatile affairs and especially vulnerable to rapid depopulation and extinction. From the very beginning, editors spent much of their time encouraging the doubters, quieting rumors of bust, and shoring up the sagging spirits of town dwellers. When times were dull this was not easy. *The Weekly Arizona Miner*, no longer able to ignore the steady exodus of people from Prescott, aired its concern: "It pains us to see pioneer citizens of the Territory throw up the sponge . . . , leave a country they know and acknowledge to be rich, and strike out, over dreary deserts, for some inflated humbug of a country, hundreds of miles away."[1] In Montana, the *Helena Herald* admitted that times were depressed at the present and many businesses were struggling to make ends meet, but it confidently predicted that within "forty days" mining activity "will have passed the impending depression and all branches of business as well as all classes of our citizens will find themselves again in full cheer under the welcome star of prosperity."[2] With similar confidence, the Black Hawk, Colorado, *Daily Mining Journal* noted that although the camp was threatened on all fronts—by mining excitements in Montana, by depressed conditions at home, by false rumor and gossip—it nevertheless counseled that "all we have to do is act firmly on the lessons of the past, and our future will be more prosperous and successful than we dare dream."[3]

No doubt these cheerful expressions of optimism belied existing conditions, but most editors did not deliberately set out to misrepresent the resources of the region. Their faith in the land and its mineral wealth was genuine and based on personal observation and study. To discredit the "croakings" of disgruntled "Gobackers" who saw nothing but humbug in the Cherry Creek diggings, William Byers of Denver's *Rocky Mountain News* personally inspected nearby mining activity and reported his findings in the first issue of his paper. Byers claimed that his "maiden effort" at panning gold not twenty miles distant from Denver City netted him about "twenty cents to two pans of earth" and that those who were working the streams along with him were averaging about two dollars a day in profits. The editor concluded by saying: "When water is brought to these diggings—which will be soon—so that sluices can be worked, the result will be great."[4] In Wyoming, the *South Pass News* strongly urged local residents to refrain from spreading inflated stories about the wealth of the Sweetwater mines and blamed "exaggerated accounts" of Colorado's mines for the present reduction in mining production that was occurring throughout the mountain West.[5] The Colorado *Caribou Post* voiced a similar concern and assured readers that all reports appearing in the *Post* about the richness of the Caribou mines should not be taken as "puffs" but rather as accurate indicators based on hard scientific fact.[6] And a Virginia City, Montana, paper allowed that it frequently used "strong language" to describe the Montana diggings, but it quickly added that "our statements are literally and exactly correct; for no temptation would induce us to prostitute our pen to the manufacture of false or inflated statements, made with a view to personal advantage. . . ."[7]

At the same time that they worked to dispell doubt about the future of the mines, editors also offered words of encouragement to local

businessmen. They commonly called attention to the many new building projects underway in and about the camp's central business district and praised merchants for their enterprising spirit. The Bozeman,
Montana, *Avant Courier* told readers that they should be proud of
the fact that "both stores and dwellings are constantly growing up;
one or two additions have been made to the site of the city, and new
streets have been opened."[8] New Mexico's *Cimarron News* proudly
made mention of the many buildings under construction in the town
and boasted that "a busier scene of the kind that is now presented . . .
could be difficult to find in any part of the United States."[9] To camp
editors, any building activity bode well for the future of the town. As
Georgetown's *Colorado Miner* expressed: "The mania for building
that pervades all classes here does not make it appear much as though
Georgetown was playing out."[10]

When business activity was slow, editors were not at all reluctant to
demand that merchants provide tangible evidence of their enterprising nature and civic pride. According to the Tucson *Daily Arizona
Star*, all businessmen were duty-bound to improve the appearance of
the city and to use every available means to finance new buildings and
stores.[11] The Montana *Missoula and Cedar Creek Pioneer*, alarmed
by the failure of businessmen to provide the miners of Cedar Creek
with adequate housing facilities, urged "Hotel Men" to pool their
resources and build the necessary accommodations.[12] A similar housing shortage in Boulder, Colorado, provoked *The Boulder County
News* to publish an open letter addressed to two of the camp's leading
lumbermen. The paper informed the men that it was their responsibility to look after the lodging needs of the community and confidently declared that "there is no investment that would pay you
better and more surely than this. Won't you go into the business?"[13]

Should such "requests" go unheeded, business leaders suffered
further abuse in the press. *The Daily Laramie Sentinel* advised repeatedly that a road should be built linking the mines of Sweetwater
to those of Helena and Virginia City, Montana.[14] When this counsel
was ignored the paper attacked civic leaders for their lack of public
spirit and scolded: "Nature has done everything for us possible . . .
but it wants a little more active energy and enterprise, well directed,
among our business men."[15] Businessmen in Boulder, Colorado, drew
even stronger fire from the *Boulder County Pioneer*. Ired by the
failure of merchants to actively exploit the nearby mountain trade,

the *Pioneer* angrily charged that "our businessmen . . . sit idly around, and let our sister towns not half so advantageously located, secure all the commerce . . . simply from a lack of public spirit."[16]

Health and sanitation facilities were also of concern to frontier journalists. Most camps were founded with almost no thought of the disposal of garbage and human waste, or of the future availability of safe drinking water. From an early date, editors urged townsfolk to use their good sense by dumping refuse in carefully selected sites away from the camp and its streams, but only rarely was this done. A Colorado editor bitterly complained about the stench caused by uncollected garbage and "unvaulted privies" and warned that unless the streets were cleaned up and a sewer constructed "a suitable location for an extensive grave-yard should be selected without delay."[17] Similar problems prevailed in Denver. Calling the city as "dirty a town as any one of its size in the country," the *Denver Daily* berated public officials for permitting "old clothes, bones, and decayed vegetable matter" to pile up in backstreets and predicted that unless immediate action was taken to rid the place of its filth, widespread sickness would be the inevitable result.[18] It was not the piles of garbage that agitated the *Laramie Daily Sentinel* but the method used to collect garbage. Noting the "herds" of hogs wandering free in the streets creating "disgusting mud holes," the *Sentinel* allowed that "we like hogs, they are good things to have in a family, town or community," but thought that fifteen hundred hogs running wild "is getting it a little too thick for either profit or pleasure."[19] Dogs not hogs concerned *The Montana Post*. Reminding residents of a city ordinance banning untended dogs in Virginia City, the *Post* called upon city authorities to summarily shoot all animals found roaming wild in the streets.[20] Once again, demands for clean streets and adequate protections against disease usually were directed to city fathers and business leaders. Editors argued that while the appearance of the town was of concern to all classes of citizens, it was the particular responsibility of merchants and those who had a significant financial investment in the camp to insure that needed improvements were realized. After all, they were the ones who stood to profit most from continued prosperity and, thus, it was their duty to see to it that the camp was an attractive and healthy place in which to live.[21]

However, general townsfolk did not escape editorial criticism. As the self-annointed guardians of good order and civilization, camp editors had much to say about the "unrefined mannerisms" of some town dwellers and offered less than subtle advice on a wide-range of topics dealing with personal behavior. Among those who received regular attention of the press were idlers and habitual loafers. Concerned about the many "deadbeats" who spent their waking hours basking in the sun or gambling for whiskey money, Virginia City's *Montana Post* reminded these "hangers-on" that unless they quickly found gainful employment, it was unlikely that they would survive the coming winter when most mining activity closed down.[22] A "bummer" in Sante Fe drew the unwelcomed attention of the *Weekly Post*. Referring to the man by the contempuous use of the "lower case," it declared that "one j. c. hill" was "too lazy to work" and warned merchants that "hill" now was attempting "to get, through some channel or other, enough to liquidate those little whiskey, billiard and board bills which keep staring him in the face."[23] In Central City, Colorado, the *Daily Miners' Register* came to the defense of a woman who was a nightly victim of her wife-beating husband. Revealing that the couple lived "not a half block from our office," the paper called the man a "brute of the lowest order" and proclaimed that "the man who will strike a woman, and that woman his wife, deserves and will receive the reprobation of the whole community."[24]

The kind and quality of camp amusements also received press notice. Papers heartily encouraged wholesome games and innocent diversions from work, but were vehement in their opposition to games that smacked of backwardness or revealed primitive tastes. *The Boulder County Pioneer* voiced its disapproval of games in which animals were abused saying that "no person of ordinary sense envies a man . . . whose delight is in horse racing, dog fighting . . . and kindred 'sports' without an aspiration for something nobler and better in life."[25] In nearby Georgetown, the *Colorado Miner* expressed disapproval when a "fat woman" was placed on display at a local theater for the curious to inspect. "We may be a little eccentric," it chided, "but we cannot see anything instructive or amusing in the sight of a big beast who seems to have been made simply for the purpose of ascertaining to what extent the human skin could be stretched without tearing."[26]

Camp editors also tried to bring a certain refinement to the language habits of their readers. They were not so naive to think they could sweep from the mining vocabulary all obscene colloquialisms, but they did attempt to quiet those speech habits that could lead to internal dissention. The spreading of rumor and gossip was considered especially harmful to the solidarity of the community. A Georgetown, Colorado, editor explained that because of the camp's small size, loose gossip could seriously disrupt friendships and warned "pervaders of rumor" to mind their own affairs.[27] Under a heading of "The Snook," Santa Fe's *Weekly New Mexican* focused attention on "those mischief makers, liars and cowards" who spent their energies spreading damaging gossip about the town and asked residents to work together to stop the activities of these disruptors of the public peace and happiness.[28] *The Arizona Citizen* in Tucson criticized the American population for its free use of such expressions as "damned greasers" when referring to Mexican residents and called upon both ethnic groups to join forces to make Tucson a better place in which to live.[29] Apparently excluding its own occasional literary outbursts, Virginia City's *Montana Post* urged locals to guard against prejudice and divisive language. "There is one piece of advice that we would give to all our people," said the paper, "and that is to avoid all general denunciations, and to eschew personal abuse as inconsistent with that innate gentility which marks the genuine American."[30]

Although many camp editors were unmarried, they nonetheless took a keen interest in the rearing of children and offered much instruction and guidance to parents. Alarmed by the crowds of children roaming Virginia City's streets smoking, swearing, and generally making a nuisance of themselves, the *Montana Post* lectured parents:

Now we would suggest to those that have charge of these youngsters to look after them—send them to school, or devise some plan to turn them from the path of vice, and avoid the miserable end that inevitably follows an ill-spent youth.[31]

The Montana Radiator in Helena was similarly provoked. Reporting that "gangs of children between the ages of five and ten" had taken to the streets insulting and verbally abusing unsuspecting passersby, the paper recommended that parents use spanking-board discipline to turn their offspring away from idleness and mischief.[32] A Colorado editor was more sublime in his advice to parents, urging them not to "have a home without flowers, with no walks, no beautiful trees, and no conveniences to illustrate to the children growing up, that cleanliness, correct habits, and a love for the beautiful, are essential requirements to living well."[33]

In their continuing crusade to uplift the moral tones of the camp, editors exerted a major effort in encouraging the introduction of those institutions that would lend the community at least the appearance of permanency. Schools, churches, legitimate theater, debating and library societies, reading rooms—all were valued not only for their civilizing effects but also as evidence that the community had arrived and was beyond the boom or bust stage.

Much of their attention centered on education and the erection of school houses where both children and adults could at least receive the rudiments of learning. According to one Montana newspaperman, "if we want empty jails, full churches, happy homes, the law of love and the love of law, let us build school houses, wherever there are a dozen children to be found."[34] In southern Colorado the *Pueblo Chieftain* was equally impressed by the benefits of education. To this paper the virtue and intelligence of a community was a direct result of the level of education of its residents and the number of schools it supported. "The *Chieftain* will ever be an earnest advocate of the public school system," it vowed, "and we know of no better time than the present to urge upon the people to foster, encourage and strengthen that system which is still in its infancy in Colorado."[35]

Once a school was built, editors insisted that it be supported and parents who failed to enroll their children were severely criticized. The Central City, Colorado, *Daily Miners' Register* observed that although school was in session, only one hundred of the camp's four hundred school-age children were attending classes. "Parents are to blame for this," said the *Register*, "they retain them at home for the work they are able to perform, or what is vastly worse, permit them to run in the streets and spend time in idle sports."[36] Disappointed by the small enrollment in Denver's school, the *Weekly Rocky Mountain News* urged both "small and large" to attend the current school term and instructed parents to "guard their conduct and conversation when at home, and our word for it, they will not hereafter have cause to regret the investment."[37]

Schoolmasters also received welcomed support from the camp press. Underpaid and often unable to afford the high cost of room and board, economic pressure frequently forced teachers to resign before the end of the school term. Worried by the high turnover of teachers in Black Hawk, Colorado, the *Daily Mining Journal* pointed out that while the camp's teachers were of the highest quality they had not been "half paid." The paper disclosed that current schoolmasters received only fifty-five dollars a month while their board bills alone came to ten dollars a week. The *Journal* then demanded that city officials take immediate steps to raise the salaries of teachers.[38]

Camp editors, however, did not campaign for the early introduction of schools simply from altruistic motives. The presence of schools in the community also was valued for the positive effect it would have on distant readers. For example, the *Santa Fe Weekly Post* admitted that it supported a public education bill not so much because it believed in the intrinsic worth of education but because the the lack of such a law had seriously undermined the efforts of lobbyists in Washington, D.C. to bring statehood to New Mexico.[39] A few years later the Silver City, New Mexico, *Mining Life* echoed this view and blamed the absence of public schools in Silver City for the discouraging immigration to southern New Mexico.[40] Schools were slow to arrive in Montana, too. *The Missoula Pioneer* advanced the opinion that because the community had failed to provide for the educational needs of children "strangers and visitors charge us with apathy and lack of interest in society," an impression, the paper pointed out, that could only retard the growth of the camp.[41] Further, camp journalists believed that the presence of schools fostered community spirit and solidarity. As one frontier editor put it: "Community is helped by school, while school is helped by community."[42]

Religion—or the lack of it—was another topic of great concern to Western journalists. The Precott *Arizona Miner* was compelled to record:

We doubt if there is in the whole land a place of equal size and prominence with Prescott, and settled by Americans, so utterly destitute of religious privileges. The Sabbath brings no invitation to public worship; the sound of the church bell is not heard, and the Sabbath school, the nursery of the church, is unknown, albeit children are numerous.[43]

When a minister made his presence known in Cimarron, New Mexico, by announcing that he would hold church services on the coming Sunday, the *News and Press* sarcastically remarked that now residents would have a "singular opportunity" to show the world that Cimarron was a God-fearing place and "prospective immigrants need have no fear that churches do not exist in New Mexico."[44] In Laramie, the editor of the *Daily Sentinel* remarked that pews usually were

filled for Sunday services, but added that few if any of the worship-
pers were men. The pious editor thought it a disgrace that family men
lounged in saloons while their wives and children attended church
and cautioned the camp's womenfolk to look after the spiritual improvement of their husbands.[45] *The Daily Mining Journal* in Black
Hawk, Colorado, saw the same back-sliding tendencies of the town's
male population: "Every one will respect you as much for visiting the
house of God," it said, "as they would if you were to lounge round
some saloon."[46]

Not only were saloons and gambling halls open on Sundays but so
too were all other businesses. Far from being a day of rest and worship, the Sabbath was a day of feverish activity; a time for residents to
purchase supplies and an opportunity for them to catch up with the
latest news. Thomas Dimsdale, editor of the *Montana Post*, remarked
that the biblical sin of Sabbath-breaking was so general in newly
discovered diggings that "a remonstrance usually produces no more
fruit than a few jocular oaths and a laugh."[47]

Nevertheless, most editors made a determined effort to encourage
business houses to close their doors on Sundays. Alfred Thomson of
the Central City, Colorado, *Tri-Weekly Miners' Register* was appalled
by the lack of "piety and outward forms of Christianity" in his camp
and called upon all merchants to encourage church attendance by
closing their shops on Sunday.[48] *The Daily Sentinel* in Larmie followed a similar approach to the problem. Expressing its disapproval
of the many businesses open on the Sabbath, the paper thought it had
the perfect solution:

If we refuse to purchase goods on Sunday, there will be none sold! If we
refuse to employ men on Sunday, there will be very little unnecessary labor
done on that day! If we keep away from the dram shops, we will save our
hard earned money, our health, and our characters; and at the same time,
aid materially in enforcing the Sunday Laws![49]

The editor of the *Rocky Mountain News* indicated the importance he
attached to church attendance and the observance of the Sabbath as
indicators of Denver's cultural level when he published an explanation of an earlier article. The *News* had flippantly referred to nearby
Golden City as a "capital city without a church," intending the remarks to be humorous. But when the editor received reports that
some readers had taken the story literally, he was quick to correct the
impression:

We see, now on a reperusal . . . that it might have been considered by distant readers, in a more serious and sober light indirectly detrimental to the place, but . . . our numerous eastern readers must remember . . . that Golden City was considered by us and our people as a model town for social and educational, as well as refined and religious advantages.[50]

Libraries, reading rooms, and lecture societies were also much sought after improvements. Even during the height of a local Indian uprising near Silver City, New Mexico, the *Grant County Herald* ventured to suggest that the time was ripe for the building of a public library and estimated that at least fifty young men were willing to support financially an organization formed for the purpose.[51] A fully-stocked library, however, was beyond the means of most camps. Thus, editors encouraged residents to loan what books and journals they had to public reading rooms where everybody could make use of them. To drum up support for such an organization, Montana's *Missoula Pioneer* declared that a well-filled reading room would not only benefit the literate population, but also would have a positive effect on the manners of the rougher elements who idled in saloons and gambling halls.[52] One Wyoming editor announced his intention to give a public lecture to raise funds for establishing a reading room in the camp and pointedly remarked that he would carefully take note of those who were in attendance.[53] Lecture societies also received enthusiastic support; indeed, many journalists were themselves skilled speakers and were in great demand on the lecture circuit. While visiting Santa Fe, W. R. Thomas, a correspondent for Denver's *Rocky Mountain News*, gave a talk on "American Literature and its Great Names." According to the *Daily New Mexican*, the lecture was "the most instructive and pleasing address which has ever been delivered here, and at once stamps its author as a gentleman of extensive literary attainments . . . and a graceful and interesting speaker. We should be pleased to have more such lecturers in our city. . . ."[54]

Nor were local theater and musical productions ignored. The inaugural performance of the Sante Fe Musical and Dramatic Association received rave reviews in the *Daily New Mexican*, the paper praising the actors for their professionalism and attention to the finer meanings of the script.[55] In Denver, the *Rocky Mountain News* was equally supportive of the camp's Musical Union and effused that:

no other of the fine arts contributes so largely to esthetic education as music. It is accessible to nearly all, and finds or creates a taste for itself everywhere.

Nor is it to be regarded as an amusement merely. It is an instrument of mental and moral culture.[56]

In their capacity as the resident cultural critic, editors took special pains to publicize and review local theater productions and dramatic readings, and, with few exceptions, were more than friendly toward any cultural attempt no matter how crude.[57]

The scriblings of local aspiring poets and essayists received their share of press notice and even, on occasion, found their way into print. Mollie Sanford, an early Denver resident and a poet of no small ability, jotted in her diary that when William Byers of the *Rocky Mountain News* sampled her verses he asked her to become a regular contributor to the "literary section" of the *News* and offered her in return a six month free subscription to the paper.[58] Not all editors were so favorably impressed. Wearied by the many hours of reading the ragged doggerels of local poets, the editor of Tucson's *Arizona Citizen* rather unkindly announced that "we want our rhymsters to be assured that our pity and charity they shall never be without, even though we have no use for their poems."[59] Having stated this, the editor went on to say that since most American poets were "discovered" in Europe those locals who harbored literary ambitions might be better received if they sent their writings abroad.[60] Still, many editors were happy to publish the material of local talent—not only did their stories and poems fill empty columns, but they also gave evidence of the camp's active, if not advanced, cultural life.

Especially in demand in every mining community was the presence of the so-called gentler sex. Mining camps, according to editors, suffered from the lack of wholesome female companionship, and frequent appeals for women to take up residence in the camps were found in the newspapers. *The Missoula Pioneer* candidly acknowledged that for some time the men of the community had been forced to seek out the "Pocahantases" of the mountains, but now because "disease and demoralization are prevalent among our . . . redskins," local bachelors had resolved to "go it alone rather than invest. The great cry now is 'send us maids and widows' and they shall be gobbled up instantly and made happy."[61] Equally anxious to see young and marriageable women arrive was the editor of Georgetown's *Weekly Colorado Miner*. After extolling the many virtues of the camp's male population, the editor asked all distant family men, especially those

with a "growing family where lovely girls are of its ambitious constit-
uents" to emigrate to Colorado. "Come," he said, "and fear not that
the voice of reason will be heard as clearly as in the quiet town or
busy city of the Atlantic."[62] The few ladies in the camp were sure to
receive their share of notice in the press. Perhaps in an attempt to stir
the blood of more than a few eastern bachelors, the *Rocky Mountain
News* waxed eloquently about the number of ladies who daily prome-
nanded in the streets

arrayed in the newest, costliest silks . . . made upon strict conformity with
the latest Paris fashion. The daintiest bonnets are gracefully appended to the
backs of their dear little heads, and butterfly parasols have shielded them for
the ardent rays of 'old sol,' for months past. . . .[63]

These efforts to elevate the moral and cultural level of the camp, to
create a community purpose and civic pride, and above all, to encourage the introduction of familiar institutions and the immigration
of permanent settlers became an all-consuming passion of early camp
journalists. If they sometimes became impatient with the backward
ways of some of the people or if their demands for improvements
became increasingly strident, it was because they had set their stand-
ards high and because they had a genuine faith in the land. Many
times their labors were in vain. But as long as there was "a shot in the
locker" they stood as the camp's most committed voice for reason and
civilization.

7

Conclusion

Small and ragged as they appeared, often printed on varying hues of paper, marred by typographical and grammatical inconsistencies, choked with stagecoach timetables and advertising of all kinds and sometimes published irregularly or occasionally, the camp press nevertheless was a major force for cultural change on the Rocky Mountain mining frontier. Between 1859, the year of the great stampede to the Pike's Peak Country, and 1881 when mining excitement in Arizona Territory once again sent thousands of prospectors into the high country, an impressive array of mountain newspapers made their appearance in the camps and gave outward evidence of the westerners' serious intent to settle and tame a new land. Not all of these papers survived and many disappeared shortly after their founding. But those that did endure became important cultural institutions in their own right. Far more than passively chronicling the day's or week's events, the mining press played an active role in civic and cultural affairs and worked tirelessly to instill a sense of pride, community, and purpose into a random and highly diverse population.

While frontier editors had much in common with their eastern brethren—a newsroom was pretty much the same wherever it was located—much separated them as well. Obviously, big-city editors with their large staffs, more technologically advanced equipment, and who worked in an environment of a long-established urban center, faced different problems than those met by their western counterparts. The large eastern city was not threatened by immediate depopulation; communication with the outside world was constant and papers faced no dearth of newsworthy items to print; churches, schools, and libraries were fixed institutions and, although acts of crime and violence often caused moments of unrest and concern, adequate protections existed for the public's safety. In such surroundings, eastern editors could devote much space in their papers to the activities of a wide-range of social groups, and they could take the time necessary to write detailed and lengthy editorials on a variety of philosophical, political, and economic issues. Even editors in country hamlets of the East worked in a relatively stable and predictable environment. Most villages were agricultural centers where life went on much as it had for generations. Here, rural editors could concentrate on gathering news items of purely local interest. Farming news and dispassionate essays were more likely to appear in these small papers than urgent exhortations against lawlessness or frantic calls for immigration.

In the mining West, however, conditions were far different. Artificially implanted on the land, without roots or traditions and without any guarantee that the diggings would prove their promise, a mining camp was as likely to go bust as it was to prosper. The appearance of these instant cities gave evidence of their temporary character. Stores and dwellings were hastily erected and haphazardly placed; dangerous mining excavations were left unattended in the winding and narrow streets; and the most prominent buildings usually were drinking and gambling emporiums. Crowded into these mining centers was a highly mobile population. Most town dwellers were transients—stampeders—who were willing to remain in the camp only as long as it held the promise for quick and easy riches. Should the diggings show signs of playing out, they were only too ready to pull up stakes and try their luck elsewhere. The activities of the saloon and gambling hall crowds also contributed to the basic instability of early mining communities. A wide-open boom camp with its unstructured and abandoned ways was an irresistible attraction for men who were accustomed to living outside the law; their presence in the camp caused considerable tension and widespread concern. Thus, while camp life had a cheerful exuberance, an undercurrent of fear and apprehension was present as well.

Despite the unsettled nature of the camps, many editors believed that these instant cities provided an ideal setting for journalistic efforts. Young men were particularly ready to test their skills on the Rocky Mountain mining frontier. That they lacked editorial experience did not matter. For the fact was that experienced editors were hard to come by in the mountain West. Few eastern editors who had families and commitments to a paper and community were willing to risk all and begin their professional careers anew in an unknown and inhospitable land. Young journeyman printers, however, usually had no such ties. Thus, with the field open, the West offered them a unique opportunity to settle down in a community and edit their own newssheets. As a result, many mining papers were operated by men with little if any editorial experience. Many of these editors were former itinerant printers, men who had worked on several eastern newspapers as typesetters and compositors but who had never entered the editorial room. Others were entirely new to the profession. School teachers, ex-miners, army officers, clergymen, speculators, Indian agents, merchants—all found editorial positions with western newssheets.

For these men of print the overriding task was to aid in bringing some semblance of order and permanency to the camps, to induce immigration, and to encourage the introduction of those economic, social, and political institutions that would at least make future growth possible. Thus, a frenzied and hurried tone, a nervous vitality, characterized the camp press but was lacking in eastern newspapers. Town dwellers were bombarded by a host of demands and urgent appeals for more housing, for better and cleaner streets, for law and order, and for the founding of schools and churches and other evidences of civilization and culture. With carrot and stick in hand, camp editors alternately praised locals for their enterprise and public spirit and berated them for their backward manners and hesitant ways. And of course, if the community were blessed with an advantage—the richness of the mines, the fertility of the soil, the mildness or therapeutic qualities of the climate—editors were quick to see its promotional value and never tired of bringing it to the attention of readers. Moreover, at a time when stateside editors were placing increased emphasis on the reporting of straight news stories, camp editors were enlarging upon the traditions of personal journalism. Throughout the 1859–1881 frontier period, early western newsmen penned their thoughts and concerns in language that was colorful, sometimes strident, and frequently explosive. This abandoned rhetoric also stamped early camp editors as a breed apart from their eastern contemporaries.

How successful they were in their self-appointed mission to bring immigration, law and order, and permanency to their community is difficult to determine with any degree of certainty. Of course, there was nothing they could do when the diggings played out and the population moved on, and many mountain newssheets were short-lived. But in those communities that prospered, editors found a fertile field for their endeavors. Not that their papers became instant financial successes—far from it. Editors were chronically short of available cash and many were forced to take extreme measures to collect the money owed them by merchants and subscribers. Nevertheless, it is clear that their newspapers reached thousands of readers weekly. Many camp papers could boast of from two hundred to a thousand subscribers, but the number of readers must have been much higher. Single copies were sold on the streets, but of even greater significance was the fact that for every issue sold there were probably half a dozen readers. Thus, for all their problems, for all their grumblings about ungrateful subscribers and financial "deadbeats," most editors enjoyed a wide readership. Outsiders, too, enlarged the circulation of the camp press. Contemporary letters and diaries testify to the fact that westerners regularly sent their local paper to friends and relatives in the East. Further, editors themselves shipped copies of their paper to eastern towns where they were sold to prospective immigrants. The many advertisements placed in mining papers by merchants from such towns as St. Louis, Omaha, Lincoln, and Leavenworth indicates that the number of these distant readers was considerable.

With a large and diverse readership and armed with a caustic pen, camp editors immediately established themselves as the community's leading booster and its most visible spokesman. Outsiders were told of the best routes to the goldfields, what supplies and equipment they should bring, the extent and richness of the mines, and the opportunities available to those who contemplated making the camp their permanent home. At the same time, editors were indefatigable in their efforts to improve camp conditions and to elevate the moral tone of the community. Their rousing appeals for an end to lawlessness, their attacks against the gambling and saloon hall crowds, and their words of encouragement for business leaders, laborers, and farmers provided a standard around which camp dwellers could rally and gave tangible expression to the young town's hopes and aspirations. While editors could in no way guarantee the survival of any boom camp, and although some of their demands for social change were not always acted upon, they did succeed in giving definition to issues that were of vital importance to all residents and their presence in the camp helped to unite westerners in a common effort to bring permanency, culture, and civilization to their adopted home.

Notes

1. The Cross-Mowry correspondence can be followed by consulting the *Washington States* as cited. The Mowry letter, written at Tucson, was dated July 2, 1859 and appeared in the *Washington States* on July 23, 1859.

The details of the duel and the written agreement by Cross and Mowry, as well as a statement prepared by the seconds are in the *Weekly Arizonian*, July 14, 1859. Eyewitness accounts appear in the *Arizona Enterprise* (Tucson), March 3, 1892; and the *Arizona Weekly Star* (Tucson), December 4, 1879.

For the position of Cross on the Arizona movement and his stance in favor of a judicial district, see the *Weekly Arizonian*, March 10, 1859, March 17, 1859, March 24, 1859, April 14, 1859, and June 30, 1859.

CHAPTER 1

1. In his report, however, Greeley warned that mining was hard, isolated work and not suited for everybody, a point many goldseekers chose to ignore. The report first appeared as an "Extra" of the *Rocky Mountain News* (Denver) and was signed by Greeley, A. D. Richardson, and Henry Villard. Details of the "Extra" and its effect are given by Robert G. Athearn, *The Coloradans* (Albuquerque: University of New Mexico Press, 1976), pp. 14–15; and Robert L. Perkin, *The First Hundred Years: An Informal History of Denver and the Rocky Mountain News* (Garden City, New York: Doubleday & Company, Inc., 1959), pp. 95–120.

2. This point is fully treated by Duane A. Smith in *Rocky Mountain Mining Camps: The Urban Frontier* (Bloomington: Indiana University Press, 1967). See also Rodman W. Paul, *Mining Frontiers of the Far West, 1848–1880* (New York: Holt, Rinehart and Winston, 1963), pp. 1–11.

3. Thomas G. Wildman to Lucy Starr Wildman, August 6, 1859 as quoted in LeRoy R. Hafen and Ann W. Hafen, eds., *Reports from Colorado: The Wildman Letters, 1859–1865. With Other Related Letters and Newspaper Reports, 1859* (Glendale, Calif.: The Arthur H. Clark Company, 1961), p. 32. Pioneer recollection literature abounds with like statements. See, for

example, Robert G. Athearn, ed., "Life in the Pike's Peak Region: The Letters of Matthew H. Dale," *The Colorado Magazine* 32 (April 1955): p. 91; Mrs. Henry Wetter to her mother, October 8, 1871, *Henry Wetter Papers*, Manuscript Collections, The Museum of New Mexico Library, Santa Fe; H. S. Hawley, *Diary*, November 5, 1860, Documentary Resources Department, State Historical Society of Colorado, Denver (hereafter cited as SHSC); Isaac Roger, *Diary*, March 10, 1865, Manuscript Collections, Montana Historical Society, Helena; and Julius E. Warton, *History of the City of Denver from its Earliest Settlements to the Present Time* (Denver: Byers and Dailey, 1866), p. 21.

4. Byers dated the first issue of the *News* April 23, although he actually went to press and distributed the paper on the evening of April 22, 1859. The founding of the *Rocky Mountain News* and the Byers-Merrick race received much attention from contemporary observers. See William N. Byers, "The Newspaper Press of Colorado," pp. 3–5 in *Hubert Howe Bancroft Scraps*, Western Historical Collections, University of Colorado Libraries, Boulder; and Byers, "History of Colorado," *Encyclopedia of Biography and History of Colorado*, I(Chicago: The Century Publishing and Engraving Company, 1901) p. 40; "Byers Interview," *The Denver Times*, December 31, 1896. Other useful eyewitness or first-hand accounts appear in A. E. Pierce, "Reminiscences of a Pioneer," *Sons of Colorado* 2(October, 1907) pp. 3–11; John L. Dailey, "Recollections," p. 2 in *Hubert Howe Bancroft Scraps*, Western History Collections, Denver Public Library (Hereafter cited as DPL); Ovando J. Hollister, *The Mines of Colorado* (Springfield, Mass.: Samuel Bowles & Company, 1867) p. 89; Frank Hall, *History of the State of Colorado*, 3(Chicago: The Blakely Printing Company, 1889), pp. 130–55; and Jerome C. Smiley, *The History of Denver; With Outlines of the Earlier History of the Rocky Mountain Country* (Denver: Times-Sun Publishing Company, 1901), pp. 247–49. Recent scholarly accounts include Edwin A. Bemis, "Journalism in Colorado," in LeRoy R. Hafen, ed., *Colorado and Its People; A Narrative and Topical History of the Centennial State*, II (New York: Lewis Historical Publishing Company, 1948), pp. 247–78; and the highly entertaining treatment by Robert L. Perkin, *The First Hundred Years*, pp. 165ff.

5. Henry Villard, *The Past and Present of the Pike's Peak Regions*, ed. LeRoy R. Hafen (Princeton: Princeton University Press, 1932), p. 151. Horace Greeley made the same observation in a dispatch to *The New York Tribune*, later published in *An Overland Journey, from New York to San Francisco, in the Summer of 1859* (New York: C. M. Saxton, Barker and Company, 1860), p. 158.

6. See D. W. Working, "Some Forgotten Pioneer Newspapers," *The Colorado Magazine* 4(May 1927):93–100.

7. Although Tubac and Tucson, Arizona, were not in the strict sense mining camps, mining excitements in the region did give birth to papers that had the same flavor as purely camp sheets.

8. Thomas G. Dimsdale, *The Vigilantes of Montana: Or Popular Justice in*

the Rocky Mountains, With an Introduction by E. De Golyer (Norman: University of Oklahoma Press, 1953), p. 6. See also Nathaniel P. Lanford, *Vigilante Days and Ways: The Pioneers of the Rockies, the Makers and Making of Montana, Idaho, Oregon, Washington and Wyoming*, with an Introduction by Dorothy M. Johnson (Missoula: Montana State University Press, 1957), pp. 89–96. A vivid, day by day account of lawlessness in a mining camp is sketched in *The Private Journal of George Whitwell Parsons, 1879–1882*. Manuscript Collections, Arizona Historical Society, Tucson.

9. Hollister, *The Mines of Colorado*, pp. 98–99.

10. *The Montana Post* (Virginia City), November 12, 1864.

11. Charles Wentworth Dilke (Sir), *Greater Britain: A Record in English-Speaking Countries During 1866 and 1867* (New York: Harper & Brothers, 1869), p. 125. Descriptions of the harsh conditions facing frontier editors are legion. For a few, see "Correspondent" to the *Daily Times* (Leavenworth, Kansas), June 4, 1859; *Mining Life* (Silver City, New Mexico), July 10, 1873; *Boulder County News* (Colorado), May 20, 1871; and the highly readable account by Albert D. Richardson, *Beyond the Mississippi: From the Great River to the Great Ocean* (Hartford, Conn.: American Publishing Company, 1873), p. 189.

12. For an excellent description of the Washington hand press and the mechanics of its operation, see Don Schellie, *The Tucson Citizen: A Century of Arizona Journalism* (Tucson: The Citizen Publishing Company, 1970), p. 15. See also "The Establishment of Journalism in Arizona, 1859–1871," (M.A. Thesis, University of Arizona, 1966), pp. 61–62.

13. *The Montana Post* (Helena), June 5, 1866.

14. *Denver City Gazette*, March 14, 1868. Virtually every frontier editor felt over-worked. See the *Weekly Arizonan* (Tucson), January 15, 1870 and *The Colorado Transcript* (Golden), May 1, 1867.

15. *The Arizona Citizen* (Tucson), June 21, 1873. W. R. Thomas, a well-travelled pioneer editor in Denver and Central City, Colorado, provides a good account of the daily activities of an editor in the *Rocky Mountain News*, April 23, 1909.

16. This is, of course, a composite picture. Many journals were published on a bimonthly, biweekly, triweekly and even an occasional basis. Most were first issued as four-page sheets and when business allowed were expanded.

17. *Weekly Commonwealth* (Denver), July 9, 1863.

18. See the *Mining Life* (Silver City, New Mexico), May 17, 1873. The editor angrily charged that a drunken freight driver had "lost" an entire shipment of paper.

19. "Byers Interview," *The Denver Times*, December 31, 1896.

20. *The Montana Post* (Virginia City), April 1, 1865.

21. Ibid. See also *The Grant County Herald* (Silver City, New Mexico), November 3, 1877; *New North-West* (Deer Lodge, Montana), October 28, 1871; *The Helena Herald* (Montana), November 15, 1866; *The Colorado Miner* (Georgetown), April 16, 1868; *The Daily Times* (Leavenworth, Kansas), July 1, 1859; Dilke, *Greater Britain*, p. 122.

22. *Daily Mining Register* (Central City, Colorado), September 7, 1866.

23. Ibid., December 4, 1864.

24. *The Daily New Mexican* (Santa Fe), July 1, 1870.

25. Ibid.

26. Frank Hall to Mrs. Emma Hall Low, June 28, 1868, *Frank Hall Papers*, DPL.

27. *Mining Life* (Silver City, New Mexico), May 17, 1873. For similar justifications see *The Sweetwater Mines* (South Pass City, Wyoming), May 27, 1868; *Tombstone Epitaph* (Arizona), May 1, 1880; *Moreno Lantern* (Elizabethtown, New Mexico), May 15, 1869 as quoted in *The Santa Fe Weekly Gazette*, May 29, 1869; *The Cimarron News* (New Mexico), June 13, 1874; *The Grant County Herald* (Silver City, New Mexico), December 11, 1880; *The Arizonian* (Tubac), March 10, 1859; *The Weekly Rocky Mountain News* (Denver, Colorado), July 23, 1859; *The Montana Post* (Virginia City), September 30, 1865; *The Daily Colorado Miner* (Georgetown), December 10, 1872; and the *Arizona Weekly Miner* (Prescott), September 21, 1864. Before William N. Byers and John L. Dailey teamed up to found the *Rocky Mountain News* in Denver in 1859, the two contemplated establishing a paper in "Burt County" somewhere in Nebraska in the winter of 1856–57. Of this projected venture Dailey stated that the purpose was to "boom the town." See "Memoranda of Ancestry," *John L. Dailey Papers*, DPL.

28. Correspondent to *Sacramento Union* as quoted in *The Santa Fe Weekly Gazette*, March 24, 1866.

29. Frank Hall to Mrs. Emma Hall Low, June 28, 1868, *Frank Hall Papers*, DPL.

30. *Weekly Rocky Mountain News* (Denver), April 23, 1859.

31. *The Weekly Independent* (Deer Lodge, Montana), October 12, 1867.

32. *Arizona Daily Star* (Tucson), May 23, 1880.

33. *Boulder County News*, (Colorado), May 31, 1871.

34. *Colorado Weekly Republican* (Denver), October 19, 1861.

35. *Boulder County News*, March 29, 1870. Henry M. Blake, an early Montana editor, remembered that during dull times the cry "Copy!" produced a "thrill of terror in the editorial breast." See his "The First Newspapers in Montana," *Contributions to the Historical Society of Montana* 5: 253–64.

36. *Colorado Weekly Republican* (Denver), November 21, 1861.

37. *Daily Rocky Mountain News*, January 4, 1866. For a nearly identical statement see the *Weekly Independent* (Helena, Montana), April 17, 1874.

38. *Weekly Arizona Miner* (Prescott), June 11, 1870.

39. *Sweetwater Mines* (South Pass City, Wyoming), June 26, 1868.

40. *Daily Mining Journal* (Black Hawk, Colorado), January 30, 1864.

41. Blake, "The First Newspapers of Montana," *Contributions to the Historical Society of Montana* 5:260.

42. *The Daily Times* (Leavenworth, Kansas), August 17, 1859.

43. Correspondent to *The Missouri Republican* (St. Louis), September 14, 1859.

CHAPTER 2

1. The phrase was coined by William N. Byers, founder of the *Rocky Mountain News* in Denver. See his "The Newspaper Press of Colorado," p. 3 in *Hubert H. Bancroft Scraps*, Western Historical Collections, University of Colorado Libraries, Boulder (Hereafter cited as CU).

2. Gibson was the brunt of much ridicule because of his pronounced English accent, a colorful description of which appears in Albert D. Richardson, *Beyond the Mississippi: From the Great River to the Great Ocean* (Hartford, Conn.: American Publishing Company, 1873), p. 297.

3. Accounts of Thomas Gibson's Colorado experience appear in George A. Crofutt, *Grip-Sack Guide of Colorado: A Complete Encyclopedia of the State* (Omaha: The Overland Publishing Co., 1881), 1:178; *The Western Mountaineer* (Golden), December 7, 1859; Byers, "The Newspaper Press of Colorado," *Bancroft Scraps*, pp. 9–10; Ovando J. Hollister, *The Mines of Colorado* (Springfield, Mass.: Samuel Bowles and Co., 1867), p. 439; Jerome C. Smiley, *History of Denver; With Outlines of the Earlier History of the Rocky Mountain Country* (Denver: The Times-Sun Publishing Company, 1901), pp. 654–56; D. W. Working, "Some Forgotten Pioneer Newspapers," *The Colorado Magazine* 4 (May 1927):100; Robert L. Perkin, *The First Hundred Years: An Informal History of Denver and the Rocky Mountain News* (Garden City, New York: Doubleday and Co., Inc., 1959), pp. 286ff; Thomas H. Ferril and Helen Ferril, eds., *The Rocky Mountain Herald Reader* (New York: William Morrow and Co., 1966), pp. 1–20; and Robert G. Athearn, *The Coloradans* (Albuquerque: University of New Mexico Press, 1976), p. 45.

4. The eldest of the Fisk brothers, Captain James Fisk, led several exploratory expeditions into the Montana goldfields. See W. Turrentine Jackson, "The Fisk Expeditions to the Montana Gold Fields," *The Pacific Northwest Quarterly*, 33 (July 1942):265–82.

5. "Memoriam," *Contributions to the Historical Society of Montana* 5: 265–72; James H. Mills, "Reminiscences of an Editor," Ibid., 272–76; and "Journal of N. H. Webster," Ibid., 3:300–30.

6. Joseph Wolff, "How the First Newspaper Came to Boulder," *Boulder Daily Camera*, February 27, 1908; James P. Maxwell, "How the First Newspaper Came to Boulder," *Boulder News and Banner*, November 1, 1887, Western History Collections, CU; *The Colorado Transcript* (Golden), April 24, 1867. See also Workers of the Writers' Program of the Work Projects Administration, *Colorado: A Guide to the Highest State* (New York: Hastings House, 1941), p. 41; Edwin A. Bemis, "Journalism in Colorado," in LeRoy R. Hafen ed., *Colorado and Its History: A Narrative and Topical History of the Centennial State* (New York: Lewis Historical Publishing Company, 1948), 2:255; and Athearn, *The Coloradans*, p. 45.

7. *Boulder County Pioneer*, February 10, 1869. For the tortured negotiations between Julius Wharton and the owners of the *Boulder County News*, see the *Colorado Miner* (Georgetown), June 25, 1868.

8. *The Daily New Mexican* (Santa Fe), October 4, 1869.

9. *Boulder County News*, April 4, 1873. For brief accounts of other journeyman printers see R. C. Brown, "Reminiscences," (typescript copy), Arizona Historical Society, Tucson; Estelle Lutrell, *Newspapers and Periodicals of Arizona, 1859–1911* (Tucson: University of Arizona Press, 1950), pp. 78–79. Lutrell's work is particularly valuable for a chapter listing the known pioneer editors in Arizona with biographical information on some of the more prominent editors. See also Henry N. Blake, "The First Newspaper of Montana," *Contribution to the Historical Society of Montana* 5:254; *Daily Arizona Miner* (Prescott), September 16, 1867; and *Santa Fe Weekly Gazaette*, June 12, 1869.

10. *U.S. Bureau of Census, 1870*, Territory of Arizona.

11. *U.S. Bureau of Census, 1870*, Boulder County, Colorado.

12. A valuable source for background on early Wyoming journalists is W. E. Chaplin, "Some of the Early Newspapers of Wyoming," *Wyoming Historical Society Miscellanies*, Western History Collections, University of Wyoming, Laramie.

13. *U.S. Bureau of Census, 1860*, Arapahoe County, Kansas Territory.

14. *Tri-Weekly Miners' Register*, July 28, 1862.

15. Ibid., April 14, 1863.

16. *The Montana Pioneer*, December 14, 1872.

17. For Collier's entrance into journalism see the anniversary edition of the *Weekly Register-Call*, July 16, 1937.

18. *Arizona Citizen*, October 23, 1877. Particulars of Wasson's background are given in Don Schellie, *The Tucson Citizen: A Century of Arizona Journalism* (Tucson: The Citizen Publishing Company, 1970), pp. 29–43.

19. *Arizona Citizen*, October 23, 1877. Accounts of other western journalistic novices can be found in the *Weekly Montanian* (Virginia City, Montana), June 4, 1874; *Daily Arizona Miner*, (Prescott), September 21, 1867; *Santa Fe Weekly Gazette*, June 12, 1869; Jo Ann Schmitt, *Fighting Editors: The Story of Editors Who Faced Six-Shooters with Pens and Won* (San Antonio: The Naylor Company, 1958) *passim;* and Norman Cleaveland, *The Morleys: Young Upstarts on the Southwest Frontier* (Albuquerque: Calvin Horn Publisher, Inc., 1971), p. 49ff.

20. Thomas Baker, "Pencil Pictures of Pioneer Pencillers," *Rocky Mountain Magazine* 2 (March 1901):541.

21. *Boulder County News*, November 2, 1869.

22. "Memoranda of Ancestry," *John L. Dailey Papers*, Western History Collections, Denver Public Library (Hereafter cited as DPL). See Also Smiley, *History of Denver*, p. 659; and Perkin, *The First Hundred Years*, p. 124. Unaccountably, Dailey received some rather harsh criticism from his contemporaries. On the occasion of Dailey's retirement from the *News* in 1870, W. R. Thomas, the paper's night editor, wrote to his father saying "I had got to dislike Mr. Dailey as a manager. . . ." See W. R. Thomas to father, November 1, 1870, *W. R. Thomas Papers*, DPL. The most severe judgment came from an aide to Hubert H. Bancroft after he had interviewed Dailey in

1884. According to the aide, Dailey was "narrow-minded, close-fisted, self-ish, unpatriotic, and really one of the smallest men in Colorado considering his position and what Colorado has done for him." See "Colorado Notes," *Hubert H. Bancroft Scraps*, Western History Collections, CU. Although his partner William Byers never criticized Dailey in writing, neither did he anywhere praise him.

23. *Daily Rocky Mountain News*, April 2, 1862.

24. Ibid.

25. *The Weekly Arizonan*, April 23, 1870. Despite her unfortunate title, *Fighting Editors: The Story of Editors Who Faced Six-Shooters with Pens and Won*, Jo Ann Schmitt provides entertaining and useful accounts of this aspect of frontier journalism.

26. Andrew Jackson Fisk, *Diary*, November 17, 1866, *Fisk Family Papers*, Montana Historical Society, Helena.

27. Ibid., November 20, 1866.

28. Robert E. Fisk to Elizabeth Chester Fisk, December 6, 1866, *Fisk Family Papers*, Montana Historical Society, Helena.

29. *Rio Abajo Weekly Press* (Albuquerque), January 20, 1863.

30. *Weekly Rocky Mountain Herald*, September 15, 1860.

31. *Daily Miners' Register*, November 10, 1867. Stanton largely has been ignored by historians. Some information about him is available in Smiley, *History of Denver*, pp. 559–60 and in the *Frederick J. Stanton Letters*, Western History Collections, DPL.

32. *The Daily New Mexican*, (Santa Fe), August 30, 1870.

33. *Santa Fe Post*, August 28, 1870.

34. Mrs. Henry Wetter to her mother, July 3, 1873, *Henry Wetter Papers*, Museum of New Mexico, Santa Fe. Sullivan remained with the *Post* until he moved to Chicago where he was involved in a shooting incident in which his opponent was killed. See *The Herald* (Silver City, New Mexico), August 19, 1876.

35. *The Madisonian* (Virginia City, Montana), August 1, 1874.

36. *Denver Daily Gazette*, July 6, 1868.

37. *Weekly Arizona Miner* (Prescott), September 2, 1871.

38. *Weekly Independent* (Deer Lodge, Montana), January 16, 1869.

39. *Weekly Rocky Mountain News*, November 24, 1859.

40. *Daily Rocky Mountain News*, November 26, 1861.

41. Ibid., September 17, 1863.

42. Useful sources indicating the extent of their political involvement are: B. Sacks, *Be It Enacted: The Creation of the Territory of Arizona* (Phoenix: Arizona Historical Foundation, 1964), p. 6ff; Lawrence Poston, III ed., "Poston vs. Goodwin: A Document on the Congressional Elections of 1865," *Arizona and the West*, 3(Winter 1961), pp. 351–54; John P. Clum, "It All Happened in Tombstone," *Arizona Historical Review* (October 1929), pp. 46–72; Porter A. Stratton, *The Territorial Press of New Mexico, 1834–1912* (Albuquerque: University of New Mexico Press, 1969), pp. 199ff; Duane A. Smith, *Rocky Mountain Mining Camps: The Urban Frontier* (Blooming-

ton: Indiana University Press, 1967), pp. 67–68; W. E. Chaplin, "Wyoming Scrapbook: Some Wyoming Editors I Have Known," *Annals of Wyoming* 18(January 1946), p. 79: *Martin Maginnis Papers*, Western Historical Collections, Montana Historical Society, Helena; Nathan B. Blumberg and Warren J. Brier, eds., *A Century of Montana Journalism* (Missoula: Mountain Press Publishing Company, 1971), *passim*.

43. W. R. Thomas to his father, January 6, 1872, *W. R. Thomas Papers*, Western History Collections, DPL.

44. Mary Clum to John P. Clum, July 1, 1879, *John P. Clum Papers*, Western History Collections, University of Arizona, Tucson.

45. Robert E. Fisk to Carl Schurz, n.d., *Fisk Family Papers*, Western History Collections, Montana Historical Society, Helena.

46. Frank Hall to Emma Hall Low, October 25, 1874, *Frank Hall Papers*, Western History Collections, DPL.

47. Ibid.

48. Frank Hall to Harper M. Orahood, April 22, 1878, *Harper M. Orahood Papers*, Western History Collections, CU.

49. Hall settled in Denver where he regrouped his personal finances and later wrote the monumental four volume (2,266 pages in all) *History of the State of Colorado . . . from 1858–1890*. See Marie M. Shinn, "Sidelights on Nineteenth Century Colorado History as Revealed by the Letters of Frank Hall" (M.A. Thesis, University of Denver, 1960), and Wallace B. Turner, "Frank Hall: Colorado Journalist, Public Servant, and Historian," *The Colorado Magazine* 53(Fall 1976), pp. 328–51.

50. *Weekly Arizona Miner* (Prescott), October 26, 1872.

51. *Rocky Mountain Herald* (Denver), May 11, 1872.

Chapter 3

1. For the price of various frontier printing offices see "South Pass News," *Hebard Collection*, University of Wyoming, Laramie; C. Patterson to Frederick J. Stanton, June 3, 1865, *Frederick J. Stanton Papers*, Western History Collection, Denver Public Library (Hereafter cited as DPL); William S. Oury, "Arizona Journalism," *Arizona Weekly Star* (Tucson), December 4, 1879; L. F. La Croix to Martin Maginnis, January 30, 1874, *Martin Maginnis Papers*, Montana Historical Society, Helena (Hereafter cited as MHS); William N. Byers, *Diary*, June 24, 1864, Western History Collection, University of Colorado Libraries, Boulder; E. A. Slack, *Scrapbook*, June 17, 1871, State of Wyoming Archives, Cheyenne; *Helena Weekly Herald*, July 9, 1868; and Don Schellie, *The Tucson Citizen: A Century of Arizona Journalism* (Tucson: The Citizen Publishing Company, 1970), p. 40.

2. *Tri-Weekly Miners' Register* (Central City), July 28, 1862.

3. See R. C. Brown, "Reminiscences," *R. C. Brown Papers*, Arizona Historical Society, Tucson; Vivian A. Paladin, ed., "Proper Bostonian, Purposeful Pioneer," *Montana, The Magazine of Western History* 14 (Autumn 1974): 38; *Daily Missouri 'Democrat*, May 5, 1860: *The Weekly Independent*

(Deer Lodge, Montana), October 19, 1867; and "From Coutant Notes," *Annals of Wyoming* 5(July 1927):38.

4. Albert D. Richardson, *Beyond the Mississippi: From the Great River to the Great Ocean* (Hartford, Conn.: American Publishing Company, 1873), p. 331.

5. *Daily Missouri Democrat*, February 22, 1860.

6. Robert G. Athearn, ed., "Life in the Pike's Peak Region: The Letters of Matthew H. Dale," *The Colorado Magazine* 32(April 1955):91.

7. Sallie R. Herndon, *Diary*, January 13, 1866 (Microfilm copy), MHS.

8. Martha Edgerton Plassmann, *Autobiography*, p. 133, MHS. For other contemporary accounts, see A. E. Pierce, "Reminiscences of a Pioneer," *Sons of Colorado* 2(September 1907):3; H. G. Hawley,*Diary*, November 5, 1860, Documentary Resources Department, State Historical Society of Colorado (Hereafter cited as SHSC); and Henry N. Blake, "The First Newspaper of Montana,"*Contributions to the Historical Society of Montana* 5:259–60.

9. "From Coutant Notes,"*Annals of Wyoming*, p. 37.

10. *Missoula and Cedar Creek Pioneer*, September 15, 1870.

11. John L. Dailey, *Diary*, April 26, 1859, DPL.

12. Mary Edgerton to her sister, November 27, 1864, *Edgerton Family Papers*, MHS.

13. For the different papers and magazines circulating in the camps see Thomas J. Wildman to Lucy Wildman, May 14, 1859 as quoted in Le Roy R. Hafen and Ann W. Hafen, eds., *Reports from Colorado: The Wildman Letters, 1859–1865*, with Other Related Letters and Newspapers Reports, 1859 (Glendale, California: The Arthur H. Clark Company, 1961), p. 32; Andrew N. Canfield, *Diary*, January 4–6, 1868, MHS; Henry Villard *The Past and Present of the Pike's Peak Gold Regions*, ed., Le Roy R. Hafen (Princeton: Princeton University Press, 1932), p. 123; and James F. Willard, "Spreading the News of the Early Discoveries of Gold in Colorado," *The Colorado Magazine* 6(May 1929): 98–104.

14. Western journals usually printed subscription terms on the first page. For the remarkable similarity in rates throughout the frontier period see *The South Pass News*, April 9, 1870; *The Cheyenne Leader*, September 10, 1867; *The Arizona Miner* (Prescott), March 9, 1864; *The Tombstone Epitaph*, May 1, 1880; *The Madisonian* (Virginia City, Montana), December 20, 1873; *Rocky Mountain Gazette* (Helena), August 18, 1866; *The Mining Life* (Silver City, New Mexico), May 17, 1873; *Weekly Rocky Mountain News*, May 7, 1859.

15. Lyle W. Dorsett, *The Queen City: A History of Denver* (Boulder, Colo.: Pruett Publishing Co., 1977), p. 1.

16. *Weekly Rocky Mountain News*, December 11, 1862.

17. *Weekly Rocky Mountain Herald* (Denver), February 1, 1868. An almost identical statement appears in the *Weekly Helena Herald*, January 9, 1868, raising the suspicion that the Denver editor "gleaned" his thoughts from the Helena paper.

18. The *News* originally was published in Elizabethtown, New Mexico, and later, after several different owners, was moved to Cimarron and Raton.

19. *Cimarron News*, (Cimarron, New Mexico), June 13, 1874.

20. *Weekly Rocky Mountain News* (Denver), October 27, 1859.

21. *Grant County Herald* (Silver City, New Mexico), July 6, 1878.

22. For the differing collection techniques, see the *Weekly Arizona Miner* (Prescott), July 30, 1870; *Th Madisonian* (Virginia City, Montana), December 20, 1873; *The Sweetwater Mines* (South Pass City, Wyoming), April 1, 1868; *Boulder County News* (Colorado), December 28, 1869; *Pueblo Chieftain* (Colorado), June 25, 1868; *Daily Mining Journal* (Black Hawk, Colorado), September 28, 1866.

23. *Daily Rocky Mountain News* (Denver), August 10, 1866.

24. John L. Dailey, *Diary*, November 24, 1859, DPL.

25. The Byers-Thomas Warren affair is treated by a contemporary observer in Frank Hall, *History of the State of Colorado* (Chicago: The Blakely Printing Company, 1889) I, pp. 235–36. A recent account is by Robert L. Perkin, *The First Hundred Years: An Informal History of Denver and the Rocky Mountain News* (Garden City, New York: Doubleday & Company, Inc., 1959), p. 174.

26. *New North-West* (Deer Lodge, Montana), October 24, 1874.

27. *The Pioneer* (Missoula), October 24, 1874.

28. *Tri-Weekly Miners' Register* (Central City, Colorado), July 28, 1862.

29. *Grant County Herald* (Silver City, New Mexico), March 5, 1876.

30. *Mesilla Times* (New Mexico), August 24, 1861. Shortly after making this claim the *Times* suspended operations. See Martin H. Hall, "The Mesilla Times: A Journal of Confederate Arizona," *Arizona and the West* 5(Winter 1963):337–51.

31. W. E. Chaplin, "Some of the Early Newspapers of Wyoming," *Miscellanies*, University of Wyoming, Laramie.

32. Blake, "The First Newspaper of Montana," p. 254. For the limited circulation of early papers see *Weekly Arizona Miner* (Prescott), December 24, 1870; *Weekly Arizonan* (Tucson), January 14, 1871; *New North-West* (Deer Lodge, Montana), July 16, 1869; *Boulder County News* (Colorado), Vol. 1, No. 52 (n.d.); and *Weekly Rocky Mountain News* (Denver), October 27, 1859.

33. *Weekly Arizona Miner* (Prescott), December 24, 1870.

34. *The Mountanian* (Virginia City), July 31, 1873.

35. See the *Colorado Weekly Republican* (Denver), November 21, 1861.

36. *The Montanian*, March 14, 1872. The same estimate was picked up by the *Helena Daily Herald*, March 18, 1872. Obviously, this figure assumes more than one reader per copy issued.

37. *Daily Rocky Mountain News* (Denver), October 29, 1860.

38. *Rocky Mountain Gold Reporter* (Mountain City, Colorado), August 6, 1859.

39. *Laramie Daily Sentinel*, June 22, 1870.

40. *The Weekly Commonwealth* (Denver), August 6, 1863.

41. *Boulder County News* (Colorado), February 2, 1872.

42. *Mesilla Times* (New Mexico), October 17, 1861.

43. *Helena Evening Herald,* December 26, 1902.

44. *Daily Rocky Mountain News,* October 25, 1866.

45. *Boulder County Pioneer* (Colorado), March 24, 1869.

46. *Weekly Colorado Miner* (Georgetown), April 28, 1870.

47. (Sir) Charles Wentworth Dilke, *Greater Britain: A Record in English-Speaking Countries during 1866 and 1867* (New York: Harper & Brothers, 1869), p. 122. See also Lawrence W. Marshall, "Early Denver History as Told by Contemporary Newspaper Advertisements," *The Colorado Magazine* 8(September 1931):161–73.

48. *Missoula Pioneer* (Montana), February 23, 1871. The same demand was made by the *Rocky Mountain Herald* (Denver), January 18, 1873.

49. *The News and Press* (Cimarron, New Mexico), January 22, 1880.

50. *Helena Daily Herald,* January 4, 1871. Among other papers victimized see the *Daily Miners' Register* (Central City, Colorado), September 12, 1866; *Arizona Silver Belt* (Globe), March 13, 1880; *Weekly Rocky Mountain News,* October 30, 1862; *Laramie Daily Sentinel,* February 9, 1871; and the *Boulder County News* (Colorado), February 9, 1872.

51. *Helena Daily Herald,* June 22, 1870.

52. *Boulder County Pioneer,* April 14, 1869. Unfortunately for the teetotaller editor, the *Pioneer* was owned by Boulder's most renowned liquor dealer. Within a few short months the editor was removed and a more agreeeable one brought in.

53. "Professor" Thomas J. Dimsdale was Montana's pioneer journalist and first school teacher. See Robert J. Goligoski, "Thomas J. Dimsdale: Montana's First Newspaper Editor," (M.A. thesis, Montana State University, 1965) *passim.* Julius E. Wharton was a well-traveled and controversial editor, having spent time with the *Colorado Miner* (Georgetown), *Boulder County Pioneer*, and the *Rocky Mountain News.*

54. A comparison between the two sources is made in Margaret Ronan, "Memoirs of a Frontier Woman: Mary C. Ronan," (M.A. thesis, Montana State University, 1932), p. 136.

55. W. E. Chaplin, "A Lifetime in Wyoming," p. 8 (Microfilm copy), Archives of the State of Wyoming, Cheyenne.

56. For attacks on merchants who sent their job work abroad see the *Daily Miners' Register* (Central City, Colorado), January 19, 1864; *Daily Rocky Mountain Gazette* (Helena), June 30, 1870; *Rocky Mountain Herald,* (Denver), September 14, 1872; *Arizona Citizen,* (Tucson), December 13, 1873.

57. See Douglas C. McMurtrie, "The Public Printing of the First Territorial Legislature of Colorado," *The Colorado Magazine* 8(March 1936):72–78; William H. Clagett to Robert E. Fisk, February 22, 1872, *William Horace Clagett Papers,* MHS.

58. Governor B. F. Potts to G. H. Williams, October 20, 1874, *Fisk Family Papers*, MHS.

59. L. F. La Croix to Martin Maginnis, December 3, 1873, *Martin Maginnis Papers*, MHS. Similar statements appear in the *Weekly New Mexican* (Santa Fe), January 2, 1864; *Denver Daily Gazette*, April 22, 1868; and *Daily Commonwealth* (Denver), May 7, 1864.

60. *The Weekly Nugget* (Tombstone, Arizona), October 2, 1879.

61. H. G. Hawley, *Diary*, August 8, 1860, Documentary Resources Department, SHSC.

62. *The Montana Post* (Virginia City), December 30, 1865. Other justifications for a neutral political position are in *The Grant County Herald* (Silver City, New Mexico), December 11, 1880; *Cheyenne Leader*, December 5, 1867; *Boulder County Pioneer* (Colorado), February 10, 1869; *Weekly Arizona Miner* (Prescott), August 31, 1872; *Arizona Citizen* (Tucson), September 21, 1878; *Canon City Times* (Colorado), October 6, 1860.

63. *Denver Daily Gazette*, January 4, 1868.

64. *Weekly Colorado Miner* (Georgetown), October 7, 1869. See also the *Canon City Times* (Colorado), September 12, 1861: *Laramie Daily Sentinel* (Wyoming), August 6, 1870; *The Montanian* (Virginia City), August 24, 1871; and the *Avant Courier* (Bozeman), August 8, 1872.

65. E. S. Wilkinson to Martin Maginnis, February 10, 1874, *Martin Maginnis Papers*, MHS. See also L. F. La Croix to Maginnis, May 17, 1874, ibid.

66. Andrew J. Fisk, *Diary*, December 21, 1866, *Fisk Family Papers*, MHS.

67. *The Weekly Arizonan* (Tucson), October 1, 1870; *The Arizona Citizen* (Tucson), October 15, 1870. The Dooner-McCormick feud is treated in Don Schellie, *The Tucson Citizen*, pp. 25–30; Kenneth Hufford, "P. W. Dooner, Pioneer Editor of Tucson," *Arizona and the West* 10(Spring 1968):25–42.

68. J. B. Chaffee to Frank Hall, August 4, 1872, *Frank Hall Papers*, CSHS. In addition to editing the *Register*, Hall was especially active in Colorado politics as secretary of the Territory of Colorado and often served as acting governor of the state. See Marie M. Shinn, "Sidelights on Nineteenth Century Colorado History as Revealed by the Letters of Frank Hall," (M.A. thesis, University of Denver, 1960) *passim;* and Wallace B. Turner, "Frank Hall: Colorado Journalist, Public Servant, and Historian," *The Colorado Magazine* 53(Fall 1976):328–51.

69. William Horace Clagett to Robert E. Fisk, May 4, 1872, *William H. Clagett Papers*, MHS.

70. *Arizona Miner* (Prescott), March 14, 1866; *The Montana Post*, November 24, 1866.

71. William N. Byers to J. B. Chaffee, January 18, 1868, *William N. Byers Papers*, Western History Collections, University of Colorado Libraries, Boulder.

72. The close relationship between Byers and Governor Evans is treated

by Lyle W. Dorsett in *The Queen City*, pp. 1–14. See also Perkin, *The First Hundred Years*, pp. 257–58.

73. Kenneth Hufford, "The Establishment of Journalism in Arizona, 1859–71," (M.A. thesis, University of Arizona, 1966), p. 2; Marvin Alisky, "Arizona's First Newspaper, *The Weekly Arizonian*, 1859," *New Mexico Historical Review* 34(April 1959):135.

74. William H. Lyon, "The Corporate Frontier in Arizona," *The Journal of Arizona History* 9(Spring 1968):3–4. See also the *Arizona Weekly Star* (Tucson), March 11, 1880.

75. *The Maxwell Land Grant Company Papers*, Box No. 147, Special Collections Department, University of New Mexico General Library, Albuquerque.

76. Ibid. See also Norman Cleaveland (with George Fitzpatrick), *The Morleys: Young Upstarts on the Southwest Frontier* (Albuquerque: Calvin Horn Publisher, Inc., 1971), pp. 84–85; and *The Daily New Mexican* (Santa Fe), October 12, 1870.

77. *Cimarron News* (New Mexico), June 13, 1874.

78. The precarious position of camp papers is explored in the following: Porter A. Stratton, *The Territorial Press of New Mexico, 1834–1912* (Albuquerque: University of New Mexico Press, 1969), *passim;* Estelle Lutrell, *Newspapers and Periodicals of Arizona, 1859–1911* (Tucson: University of Arizona Press, 1950); D. W. Working, "Some Forgotten Pioneer Newspapers," *The Colorado Magazine* 4(May 1927);93–100; Edwin A. Bemis, "Journalism in Colorado," in Le Roy R. Hafen, ed., *Colorado and Its People: A Narrative and Topical History of the Centennial State* (New York: Lewis Historical Publishing Company, Inc., 1948)2:247–78; Jay Gurian, "Sweetwater Journalism and Western Myth," *Annals of Wyoming* 36(April 1964):79–88; Douglas C. McMurtrie, "Pioneer Printing in Wyoming," *Annals of Wyoming* 9(January 1933):729–42; Samuel A. Bristol, "The Newspaper Press of Wyoming," (photostat copy), *Hubert H. Bancroft Scraps*, Western History Collections, University of Colorado Libraries, Boulder; Albert Franklin Banta, "Arizona Newspapers: Past and Present," Department of Library and Archives, State of Arizona, Phoenix; Robert L. Houseman, "The Beginnings of Journalism in Frontier Montana," *Frontier and Midland* 15(Summer 1935): 3–10; Robert L. Houseman, "The Frontier Journals of Western Montana," *The Pacific Northwest Quarterly* 29(July 1938): 269–76; Robert L. Houseman, "Pioneer Montana's Journalistic 'Ghost' Camp—Virginia City," *The Pacific Northwest Quarterly* 29(January 1938):53–59.

79. *Colorado Miner* (Georgetown), December 17, 1868.

80. *Daily Mining Journal* (Black Hawk, Colorado), November 28, 1866.

81. *Weekly Arizonan* (Tucson), August 7, 1869. See Hufford, "P. W. Dooner, Pioneer Editor of Tucson," *Arizona and the West*, pp. 25–42.

82. *The Arizona Citizen* (Tucson), October 4, 1873.

83. Chaplin, "Some of the Early Newspapers of Wyoming," *Miscellanies*, University of Wyoming, Laramie.

84. As quoted in Schellie, *The Tucson Citizen*, p. 40; *The Arizona Citizen*, October 4, 1873.

85. *Helena Daily Herald*, Vol. 6, No. 142, n.d.; Andrew J. Fisk, *Diary*, October 1, 1871, *Fisk Family Papers*, MHS.

86. Frank Hall to Emma Hall Low, October 24, 1875, *Frank Hall Papers*, Western History Collection, DPL. See also Frank Hall to Harper M. Orahood, April 22, 1878, *Harper M. Orahood Papers*, Western History Collection, University of Colorado Libraries, Boulder.

87. John L. Dailey, "Recollection," October, 1888 (microfilm extract) in *Hubert H. Bancroft Scraps*, Western History Collection, DPL.

CHAPTER 4

1. The term "cotemporary" rather than "contemporary" was used by the camp press, apparently a humorous reference to the short life expectancy of many mountain journals.

2. *The Montana Post* (Virginia City), May 20, 1865.

3. *The Rocky Mountain Herald* (Denver), May 2, 1868.

4. *New North-West* (Deer Lodge, Montana), August 31, 1872. Contrary to the paper's prediction, the *Gazette* never recovered from the effects of the fire and eventually suspended operations.

5. Ibid., July 16, 1869.

6. See the *Daily Mining Journal* (Black Hawk, Colorado), May 23, 1864. Shortly after the destruction of the *News*, editor Byers bought out the entire plant of the *Commonwealth*, thus bringing to a close the long rivalry between the two papers.

7. *Daily Rocky Mountain News* (Denver), May 4, 1868.

8. *The Montana Post* (Virginia City), February 17, 1866.

9. Frank Luther Mott, *American Journalism, A History: 1690–1960* (3rd ed. rev.; New York: The Macmillan Company, 1962), pp. 146–47; Sidney Kobre, *Development of American Journalism* (Dubuque, Iowa: Wm. C. Brown Co. Publishers, 1969), pp. 109–40; Leary Lewis, *That Rascal Freneau: A Study in Literary Failure* (New York: Octagon Books, Inc., 1964), pp. 188–90; Leonard W. Levy, *Legacy of Supression; Freedom of Speech and Press in Early American History* (Cambridge, Mass.: The Belknap Press of Harvard University Press, 1960), pp. 267, 297–300; Allan Nevins, *The Evening Post: A Century of Journalism* (New York: Russell & Russell, 1968), p. 13; Arthur M. Schlesinger, *Prelude to Independence: The Newspaper War on Britain, 1764–1776* (New York: Alfred A. Knopf, 1958), pp. 296–301.

10. Alexis De Tocqueville, *Democracy in America*, Richard D. Heffner, ed., (New York: The New American Library, 1956), pp. 4.

11. James Melvin Lee, *History of American Journalism* (New York: Houghton Mifflin Company, 1917), pp. 321–22. The rise of the penny press and the era of personal journalism is described in Mott, *American Journalism*, pp. 292–302; Edwin Emery, *The Press and America: An Interpretative*

History of the Mass Media (3rd ed. rev.: Englewood Cliffs, New Jersey: Prentice Hall, Inc., 1972), pp. 169ff; Clement Eaton, *The Growth of Southern Civilization, 1790–1860* (New York: Harper Torchbooks, 1961), p. 268; Daniel J. Boorstin, *The Americans: The National Experience* (New York: Vintage Books, 1965), pp. 124–34.

12. (Sir) Charles Wentworth Dilke, *Greater Britain: A Record in English-Speaking Countries during 1866 and 1867* (New York: Harper & Brothers, 1869), p. 121.

13. Bayard Taylor, *Colorado: A Summer Trip* (New York: G. P. Putnam and Son, 1867), p. 60.

14. Ibid.

15. *The Montana Post* (Helena), June 12, 1868.

16. John Gregory Bourke, *On the Border with Crook* (New York: C. Scribner Sons, 1891), p. 95. For general comments on press battles see Don Schellie, *The Tucson Citizen: A Century of Arizona Journalism* (Tucson: The Citizen Publishing Company, 1970), pp. 31–35; W. E. Chaplin, "Some of the Early Newspapers of Wyoming," *Wyoming Historical Society Miscellanies*, University of Wyoming, Laramie, pp. 23–24; William N. Byers, "The Newspaper Press of Colorado," p. 5 in *Hubert H. Bancroft Scraps*, Western Historical Collection, University of Colorado Libraries, Boulder; Kenneth Hufford, "P. W. Dooner, Pioneer Editor of Tucson," *Arizona and the West* 10(Spring 1968):33–34; Robert L. Houseman, "Pioneer Montana's Journalistic 'Ghost' Camp—Virginia City," *The Pacific Northwest Quarterly* 29(January 1938):53.

17. *Helena Weekly Herald*, June 17, 1869. Similar observations appear in the *Rocky Mountain Herald* (Denver), October 21, 1871 and February 3, 1872; Byers, "The Newspaper Press of Colorado," p. 18; Bourke, *On the Border*, p. 94.

18. Bourke, *On the Border*, p. 94. Bourke used *Arizonian*, the original spelling of the paper.

19. Letter of Matthew H. Dale to his parents, April 28, 1861 in Robert G. Athearn, ed., "Life in the Pike's Peak Region: The Letters of Matthew H. Dale," *The Colorado Magazine* 32(April 1955):101.

20. *Daily Rocky Mountain News* (Denver), December 10, 1860.

21. *Weekly Montana Post* (Virginia City), December 8, 1866.

22. For example, see *The New North-West* (Deer Lodge, Montana), June 21, 1873.

23. *Weekly Rocky Mountain News* (Denver), July 23, 1863. *The Tri-Weekly Miners' Register* in Central City also noted the *Herald's* tactic. See the issue of July 16, 1863.

24. Details of the "pony express war" are given in the *Weekly Commonwealth* (Denver), July 9, 16, 1863. See also Byers. "The Newspaper Press of Colorado," pp. 11–12; Julius E. Wharton, *History of the City of Denver from its Earliest Settlement to the Present Time* (Denver: Byers and Dailey, 1866), p. 87; George A. Crofutt, *Crofutt's Grip-Sack Guide of Colorado: A Complete Encyclopedia of the State* I (Omaha: The Overland Publishing

Co., 1881), p. 178; Jerome C. Smiley, *History of Denver* (Denver: The Times-Sun Publishing Company, 1901), p. 658.

25. *Missoula Pioneer*, February 2, 1871.

26. *The News and Press* (Cimarron, New Mexico), November 20, 1879.

27. *Rocky Mountain Herald* (Denver), September 1, 1860.

28. *Weekly Arizona Miner* (Prescott), August 29, 1868.

29. *Santa Fe Weekly Post*, July 9, 1870.

30. *Helena Weekly Herald*, February 7, 1867.

31. *The Montana Post* (Virginia City), February 2, 1867.

32. *Canon City Times* (Colorado), August 29, 1861. See also the *Weekly Colorado Republican* (Denver), October 12, 1861.

33. *Arizona Citizen* (Tucson), July 12, 1873.

34. *Daily Rocky Mountain News* (Denver), June 1, 1869.

35. *The Sweetwater Mines* (South Pass City, Wyoming), April 1, 1868.

36. Ibid.

37. *Helena Weekly Herald*, September 3, 1868. For other expressions of sectional jealousies see *The Arizonian* (Tubac), April 21, 1859; *Santa Fe Weekly Gazette*, April 24, 1869; *Colorado Weekly Miner* (Georgetown), January 13, 1870; *Colorado Transcript* (Golden), August 21, 1867; *Pueblo Chieftain* (Colorado), July 9, 1868; *Cheyenne Leader*, January 23, 1868; *Missoula and Cedar Creek Pioneer* (Montana), December 22, 1870.

38. *Daily Rocky Mountain News* (Denver), October 8, 1860.

39. A lively account of the Byers-Gibson feud can be found in Robert L. Perkin, *The First Hundred Years: An Informal History of Denver and The Rocky Mountain News* (Garden City, New York: Doubleday & Company, Inc., 1959), pp. 192ff. For Gibson's retirement see the *Daily Commonwealth* (Denver), January 1 and April 12, 1864; and *Daily Miners' Register* (Central City), June 29, 1864.

40. *New North-West* (Deer Lodge, Montana), August 26, 1870.

41. *Daily Mining Journal* (Black Hawk, Colorado), September 25, 1866.

42. *Daily Rocky Mountain News* (Denver), October 7, 1868.

43. See for example, *Rocky Mountain Herald* (Denver), February 15, 1868; *Pueblo Chieftain* (Colorado), December 24, 1868; *Daily Miners' Register* (Central City, Colorado), July 17, 1867.

44. W. E. Chaplin, "Wyoming Scrapbook: Some Wyoming Editors I Have Known," *Annals of Wyoming* 18(January 1946): 80–81. See also Chaplin's "Some of the Early Newspapers of Wyoming," p. 23 of *Wyoming Historical Society Miscellanies*, University of Wyoming, Laramie.

45. *Laramie Daily Sentinel*, May 11, 1870.

46. *Daily New Mexican* (Santa Fe), April 21, 1870.

47. *Weekly Arizona Miner* (Prescott), March 26, 1870.

48. *Daily Miners' Register* (Central City, Colorado), January 4, 1867.

49. See the *Daily New Mexican* (Sante Fe), October 6, 1870; *Weekly Arizona Miner* (Prescott), November 1, 1873; *Daily Mining Journal* (Black Hawk, Colorado), May 16, 1865; *Colorado Miner* (Georgetown), February 17, 1869; *Pueblo Chieftain* (Colorado), November 4, 1869; *Cheyenne Leader*,

December 10, 1867; *Daily Helena Herald*, March 23, 1874; *The Montana Post* (Virginia City), November 18, 1865; *Weekly Independent* (Deer Lodge, Montana), February 8, 1868.

50. *Weekly Montana Post* (Virginia City), January 19, 1867.

51. *The Arizona Citizen* (Tucson), March 4, 1871; *Weekly Arizona Miner* (Prescott), January 18, 1868; *Weekly Arizonan* (Tucson), June 26, 1869; *Arizona Sentinel* (Yuma), March 29, 1873; *Santa Fe Weekly Gazette*, December 8, 1866; *Mining Life* (Silver City, New Mexico), May 9, 1874; *Daily New Mexican* (Santa Fe), November 28, 1870; *Daily Miners' Register* (Central City, Colorado), July 25, 1867; *Daily Mining Journal* (Black Hawk, Colorado), December 22, 1863; *Daily Commonwealth* (Denver), January 14, 1864; *Laramie Daily Sentinel*, June 17, 1870; *The Montana Post* (Virginia City), May 12, 1866; *Weekly Montanian* (Virginia City), September 4, 1871; *Rocky Mountain Gazette* (Helena), September 29, 1866; *Weekly Independent* (Deer Lodge, Montana), November 7, 1868.

52. *Daily Arizona Citizen* Tucson), May 6, 1880. The following issues indicate the intensity of the war; *Arizona Weekly Star*, May 6, 7, 1880 (although the *Star* was a weekly paper, when events dictated it, it was often published on a daily basis); *Daily Arizona Citizen*, May 3, 5, 6, 7, 1880.

53. *Helena Weekly Herald*, September 12, 1867.

54. *Daily Rocky Mountain News*, July 27, 1865.

55. Ibid., September 14, 1865.

56. Ibid., September 15, 1865.

57. See for details Lyle W. Dorsett, *The Queen City: A History of Denver* (Boulder, Colo.: Pruett Publishing Company, 1977). pp. 3 and 15.

58. Only a few scattered issues of the *Denver Daily Gazette* are extant during the period of the Byers-Stanton affair. For reactions by other journalists see *The Colorado Transcript* (Golden), August 28, 1867; *Daily Mining Journal* (Black Hawk, Colorado), September 16, 1865; *The Montana Post* (Virginia City), October 7, 1865. See also Perkin, *The First Hundred Years*, p. 296.

59. *Helena Daily Herald*, March 4, 1870.

CHAPTER 5

1. Some of these stories have been collected by Marvin Lewis, ed., *The Mining Frontier: Contemporary Accounts from the American West in the Nineteenth Century* (Norman: University of Oklahoma Press, 1967), pp. 1–80. See also Rodman W. Paul, *California Gold: The Beginning of Mining in the Far West* (Lincoln: Unversity of Nebraska Press, Bison Books, 1964), pp. 69–90; and the same author's *Mining Frontiers of the Far West, 1848–1880* (New York: Holt, Rinehart and Winston, Inc., 1963), pp. 1–36.

2. Two essentials contemporary accounts of the activities of the Plummer gang by on-the-scene witnesses are Thomas J. Dimsdale, *The Vigilantes of Montana; or Popular Justice in the Rocky Mountains*, With an Introduction by E. De Golyer (Norman: University of Oklahoma Press, 1953); and Nathan-

iel Pitt Lanford, *Vigilante Days and Ways: The Pioneers of the Rockies, the Makers and Making of Montana, Idaho, Oregon, Washington, and Wyoming*, With an Introduction by Dorothy M. Johnson (Missoula: Montana State University Press, 1957). Among the many secondary treatments see Paul, *Mining Frontiers of the Far West*, p. 67; and a very concise but accurate account by Daniel J. Boorstin, *The Americans: The National Experience* (New York: Vintage Books, 1965), pp. 87–90.

3. Alexander T. Rankin to Mrs. Kelly, August 10, 1860 as quoted in Nolie Mumey, ed., *Alexander Taylor Rankin: His Diary and Letters* (Boulder, Colo.: Johnson Publishing Co., 1966). Other contemporary descriptions of lawlessness in Denver appear in Albert D. Richardson, *Beyond the Mississipi: From the Great River to the Great Ocean* (Hartford, Conn.: American Publishing Company, 1873), pp. 177–78; Horace Greeley, *An Overland Journey, from New York to San Francisco in the Summer of 1859* (New York: C.M. Saxton, Barker and Company, 1860), p. 159; Mollie E. Dorsey Sanford, "Dairy," *Denver Westerners Posse Brand Book* 10(1954): 315; Irving W. Stanton, *Sixty Years in Colorado: Reminiscences and Reflections of a Pioneer of 1860*, With an Introduction by Thomas F. Dawson (Denver: By the Author, 1922), pp. 51–52; Augustus Wildman to Lucy Starr Haskins, December 16, 1860 as quoted in Le Roy R. Hafen and Ann W. Hafen, eds., *Reports from Colorado: The Wildman Letters, 1858–1865. With Other Related Letters and Newspapers Reports, 1859* (Glendale, Calif.: The Arthur H. Clark Company, 1961), pp. 271–72; Julius E. Wharton, *History of the City of Denver from its Earliest Settlement to the Present Time* (Denver: Byers and Dailey, 1866), p. 39; and Frank Hall, *History of the State of Colorado* (Chicago: The Blakely Printing Company, 1889), I, p. 221.

4. *Cimarron News*, n.d., as quoted in the *Republican Review* (Albuquerque, New Mexico), August 3, 1872. See also Norman Cleaveland, *The Morleys: Young Upstarts on the Southwest Frontier* (Albuquerque: Calvin Horn Publisher, Inc., 1971), pp. 114-19; and Porter A. Stratton, *The Territorial Press of New Mexico, 1834–1912* (Albuquerque: University of New Mexico Press, 1969), pp. 180–90.

5. *Montana Post* (Virginia City), January 28, 1865.

6. Ibid.

7. *The Tribune* (Silver City, New Mexico), December 6, 1873.

8. *Tombstone Epitaph* (Arizona), March 27, 1882.

9. *Daily Miners' Register* (Central City, Colorado), March 4, 1864.

10. *Pueblo Chieftain* (Colorado), June 25, 1868.

11. *Laramie Daily Sentinel*, July 11, 1870. For a sampling of other examples of self-censorship by the camp press see *The Santa Fe Weekly Post*, September 16, 1871; *The Weeky Arizona Miner* (Prescott), June 11, 1870; *The Arizona Citizen* (Tucson), November 16, 1872; *Weekly Rocky Mountain News* (Denver), June 11, 1859; *Daily Rocky Mountain News*, March 15, 1861; *Canon City Times* (Colorado), February 16, 1861; *The Colorado Republican* (Denver), February 20, 1862; *Weekly Rocky Mountain Herald* (Denver), August 11, 1860; *Missoula and Cedar Creek Pioneer* (Montana), Sep-

tember 22, 1870. See also Oliver La Farge, *Santa Fe: The Autobiography of a Southwestern Town* (Norman: University of Oklahoma Press, 1959), p. xii; Jay P. Gurian, "Sweetwater Journalism and Western Myth," *Annals of Wyoming* 36(April 1964): 79–88; and Gurian, "Two Western Mining Communities: A Study of their Actual Development and their Mythology," (Ph.D. diss. University of Minnesota, 1964), pp. 138–59.

12. *Daily Miners' Register* (Central City, Colorado), September 29, 1866.

13. *Cimarron News*, n.d., as quoted in *The Daily New Mexican* (Santa Fe), October 16, 1871.

14. *The Weekly Arizona Miner* (Prescott), February 22, 1873. The young man was found guilty of public drunkenness and assessed a fine of $50 and court costs. For a few of the many papers that printed names of town toughs see *The Weekly Arizonian* (Tucson), February 7, 1869; *The Arizona Citizen* (Tucson), January 13, 1872; *The Grant County Herald* (Silver City, New Mexico), December 1, 1877; *The Santa Fe Weekly Post*, December 18, 1869; *Daily Miners' Register* (Central City, Colorado), February 15, 1867; *The Montana Post* (Virginia City), December 24, 1864. For public reaction to name-posting, see A. E. Pierce, "Reminiscences of a Pioneer," *Sons of Colorado* 2(October 1907):7; and Hall, *History of the State of Colorado*, I, p. 241.

15. See especially *The Mining Life* (Silver City, New Mexico), September 27, 1873; *News and Press* (Cimarron, New Mexico), September 9, 1880; *The Colorado Miner* (Georgetown), July 9, 1868; and *The Pueblo Chieftain* (Colorado), October 22, 1868.

16. Lyle W. Dorsett, *The Queen City: A History of Denver* (Boulder, Colo.: Pruett Publishing Company, 1977), pp. 8–9.

17. *Arizona Weekly Star* (Tucson), June 13, 1878.

18. *Canon City Times* (Colorado), February 23, 1861.

19. *South Pass News* (Wyoming), April 26, 1871.

20. *Daily Tombstone Nugget* (Arizona), July 12, 1881.

21. *The Montana Post* (Virginia City), November 12, 1864. "Hurdy-Gurdy" houses usually were dancing establishments where the men bought tickets for the privilege of dancing with the ladies. In some camps, the "ladies" often were available for other forms of entertainment.

22. *Daily Miners' Register* (Central City, Colorado), July 26, 1867.

23. *Boulder County Pioneer* (Colorado), March 24, 1869. Julius E. Wharton, journalist, historian, and part-time physician, was at this time editor of the *Pioneer* and was alternately known for his violent opposition against liquor in all its forms and for his well-publicized bouts with the bottle.

24. *The Tribune* (Silver City, New Mexico), October 11, 1873. Other demands for curbing gambling and drinking can be found in *News and Press* (Cimarron, New Mexico), July 15, 1880; *New Southwest and Grant County Herald* (Silver City, New Mexico), July 30, 1881; R. A. Carple, "Reminiscences," Manuscript Collections, Arizona Historical Society, Tucson; John Gregory Bourke, *On the Border With Crook* (New York: C. Scribner Sons, 1891), p. 95; Stratton, *The Territorial Press of New Mexico*, pp. 191–93;

Weekly Colorado Miner (Georgetown), November 9, 1871; *Daily Common-wealth* (Denver), May 13, 1864; *Daily Miners' Register* (Central City, Colo-rado), August 25, 1867; *Boulder County News* (Colorado), November 8, 1872; *Daily Rocky Mountain News* (Denver), May 25, 1868; *Sweetwater Mines* (South Pass City, Wyoming), May 27, 1868; *Laramie Daily Sentinel*, September 27, 1870; *The Montana Post* (Virginia City), December 3, 1864 and March 17, 1866; *The Montana Radiator* (Helena), February 24, 1866; *The Pioneer* (Missoula, Montana), September 14, 1872; and Dimsdale, *Vigilantes of Montana*, pp.9–12.

25. *Weekly Colorado Miner* (Georgetown), November 9, 1871. See also the *Daily Colorado Miner*, January 27, 1873.

26. *New North-West* (Deer Lodge, Montana), November 26, 1869.

27. *Weekly Rocky Mountain News* (Denver), November 6, 1862.

28. *Weekly Commonwealth* (Denver), November 6, 1862.

29. *Laramie Daily Sentinel*, December 6, 1870.

30. *Daily Miners' Register* (Central City, Colorado), January 11, 1865. *The Register's* intemperate remarks came only weeks following the Sand Creek Massacre, in which Col. John M. Chivington led a contingent of Colorado militiamen in an attack upon a peaceful encampment of Cheyenne and Arapaho Indians. An estimated 600 Indians were killed and many of the bodies brutally mutilated. The engagement almost immediately became the topic of a heated nationwide controversy. For an excellent treatment of the affair see Robert L. Perkin, *The First Hundred Years: An Informal History of Denver and The Rocky Mountain News* (Garden City, New York: Doubleday & Company, Inc., 1959); pp. 253–84.

31. *Sweetwater mines* (South Pass City, Wyoming), March 28, 1868.

32. *The Montana Post* (Virginia City), May 25, 1867.

33. *The Colorado Transcript* (Golden), June 5, 1869. The camp press abounds in demands for the extermination of the western tribes. See the *Montana Post* (Virginia City), July 21, 1866; *South Pass News* (Wyoming), April 9, 1870; *Laramie Daily Sentinel*, May 14, 1870; *Weekly Rocky Mountain News* (Denver), March 26, 1863; *The Denver Daily*, February 23, 1867; *Daily Mining Journal* (Black Hawk, Colorado), January 15, 1864; *The Arizonian* (Tubac), April 21, 1859; *Grant County Herald* (Silver City, New Mexico), October 20, 1877. Useful secondary accounts are Lawrence M. Kennedy, "The Colorado Press and the Red Man: Local Opinion About Indian Affairs, 1859–1870" (M.A. thesis, University of Denver, 1967), p. 218 and *passim;* and Elmo Scott Watson, "The Indian Wars and the Press, 1866–1867," *Journalism Quarterly* 17 (December 1940);301–12; and Stratton, *The Territorial Press of New Mexico*, pp. 119–20.

34. *Weekly Colorado Republican* (Denver), May 25, 1861.

35. *Weekly Commonwealth* (Denver), November 20, 1862. *The Commonwealth* was the successor to the *Weekly Colorado Republican*.

36. The Byers kidnapping and its aftermath was one of the major events of early Colorado history and accordingly, received much attention from contemporary observers and historians alike. What has never been explained,

however, is the lasting friendship that developed between Byers and Harrison. Even in later life, after Harrison had been killed in the Civil War fighting on the Confederate side, Byers defended the former gambler and gunman. Byers has left several vivid descriptions of the affair: see the *Weekly Rocky Mountain News*, August 1, 1860; "Byers' Scraps: History of Colorado," pp. 67–68 in *Hubert Howe Bancroft Scraps*, Western History Collection, University of Colorado Libraries, Boulder; Byers, "History of Colorado," in *Encyclopedia of Biography of Colorado* (Chicago: The Century Publishing and Engraving Company, 1901), pp. 57–58; *The Denver Times*, December 31, 1896. Eyewitness and contemporary accounts include John L. Dailey, "Diary," July 31, 1860, *John L. Dailey Papers*, Western History Collections, Denver Public Library; Mumey, ed., *Alexander Taylor Rankin*, Rankin "Diary," August 1, 1860 and August 2, 1860 and letter to Mrs. Kelley, August 10, 1860; *The Daily Times* (Leavenworth, Kansas), December 13, 1860; Stanton, *Sixty Years in Colorado*, pp. 51–52; Pierce, "Reminiscences of a Pioneer," pp. 7–8; Hall, *History of the State of Colorado*, I, pp. 241–43; Wharton, *History of Denver*, p. 180; and Ovando J. Hollister, *The Mines of Colorado* (Springfield, Mass.: Samuel Bowles & Company, 1867), pp. 95–96. An invaluable source and one that is based on personal interviews with Byers and first-hand witnesses is Jerome C. Smiley, *History of Denver; With Outlines of the Earlier History of the Rocky Mountain Country* (Denver: The Times-Sun Publishing Company, 1901), pp. 345–46. More recent accounts are Perkin, *The First Hundred Years*, pp. 179–84; and Dorsett, *The Queen City*, p. 30.

37. There are no extant issues of the *Rocky Mountain Herald* for this period. For details of the attack, see the *Daily Rocky Mountain News*, February 13, 1862; and Augustus Wildman to his father, February 14, 1862 as quoted in Hafen and Hafen, *Reports from Colorado*, p. 308.

38. *The News and Press* indeed was effectivey silenced. Not until new owners arrived months following the blast was there any attempt to recount the events leading to the affair. The details given are very sparse and the causes of the affair remain a mystery. See Cleaveland, *The Morleys*, pp. 117–18. For other newspapers that sustained attack or reported attacks on neighboring papers see *The Weekly Arizona Star* (Tucson), April 10, 1879; *The Weekly Arizona Miner* (Prescott), October 26, 1872; *The Weekly Arizonan* (Tucson), December 18, 1869; *Daily Tombstone Nugget* (Arizona), November 3, 1881; *The Mining Life* (Silver City, New Mexico), May 9, 1874; *Daily New Mexican* (Santa Fe), December 1, 1870; *Daily Missouri Democrat* (St. Louis), April 15, 1859; *The Moreno Lantern* (Elizabethtown), New Mexico), n.d., as quoted in *The Daily Rocky Mountain News* (Denver), August 9, 1869; *Boulder County Pioneer* (Colorado), April 14, 1869; *The Colorado Miner* (Georgetown), July 2, 1868; *The Cheyenne Leader*, October 1, 1867; and *The Montana Post* (Helena), March 9, 1869.

39. *Daily Helena Herald*, November 6, 1871.

40. *Santa Fe Weekly Gazette*, March 19, 1859.

41. *Daily Commonwealth* (Denver), May 5, 1864.

42. Dimsdale, *The Vigilantes of Montana*, p. 16.

43. *Weekly Rocky Mountain News*, May 14, 1859.

44. Ibid., May 28, 1859.

45. Ibid.

46. *Daily Mining Journal* (Black Hawk, Colorado), December 18, 1863.

47. *Laramie Daily Sentinel*, December 13, 1870.

48. *Sweetwater Mines* (South Pass City, Wyoming), December 2, 1868.

49. *New North-West* (Deer Lodge, Montana), January 28, 1870.

CHAPTER 6

1. *Weekly Arizona Miner* (Prescott), February 20, 1869.

2. *Helena Herald* (Montana), June 12, 1867.

3. *Daily Mining Journal* (Black Hawk, Colorado), February 8, 1864.

4. *Weekly Rocky Mountain News* (Denver), April 23, 1859.

5. *South Pass News* (Wyoming), September 2, 1869.

6. *Caribou Post* (Colorado), August 19, 1871.

7. *Montana Post* (Virginia City), September 30, 1865. For warnings to avoid exaggeration see *The News and Press* (Cimarron, New Mexico), December 23, 1880; *Weekly Rocky Mountain Herald* (Denver), June 2, 1860; Letter of Frank Hall to Emma Hall Low, June 28, 1868, *Frank Hall Papers*, Documentary Resources Department, Colorado State Historical Society, Denver; *Laramie Daily Sentinel* (Wyoming), May 1, 1871; *Rocky Mountain Gold Reporter* (Mountain City, Colorado), August 6, 1859; *Daily Rocky Mountain Gazette* (Helena, Montana), August 7, 1870; and *The Montanian* (Virginia City), November 2, 1871.

8. *Avant Courier* (Bozeman, Montana), September 27, 1871.

9. *Cimarron News* (New Mexico), as quoted in the *Republican Review* (Albuquerque), November 4, 1871.

10. *Colorado Miner* (Georgetown), June 20, 1867. Other like statements appear in *The News and Press* (Cimarron, New Mexico), June 3, 1880; *Arizona Citizen* (Tucson), May 19, 1873; *Arizona Weekly Star* (Tucson), October 17, 1878; *Canon City Times* (Colorado), November 10, 1860; *Colorado Transcript* (Golden), March 13, 1867; *Daily Miners' Register* (Central City, Colorado), September 21, 1865; *Weekly Rocky Mountain News* (Denver), May 14, 1859; *Laramie Daily Sentinel* (Wyoming), July 19, 1870; *Helena Weekly Herald* (Montana), November 15, 1866.

11. *Arizona Daily Star* (Tucson), April 24, 1880.

12. *Missoula and Cedar Creek Pioneer* (Montana), October 20, 1870.

13. *Boulder County News* (Colorado), May 20, 1871.

14. *Laramie Daily Sentinel* (Wyoming), May 3, 1870.

15. Ibid.

16. *Boulder County Pioneer* (Colorado), February 17, 1869. For other press comment on merchants see the *Grant County Herald* (Silver City, New Mexico), August 3, 1878; *Santa Fe Weekly Post*, December 18, 1869; *Daily Colorado Miner* (Georgetown), Vol. 1, No. 14 (n.d.); *Daily Mining*

Journal (Black Hawk, Colorado), September 29, 1865; *Laramie Daily Sentinel* (Wyoming), May 14, 1870; *Weekly Independent* (Deer Lodge, Montana), October 12, 1867; and *Helena Daily Herald* (Montana), January 3, 1874. For contemporary reactions to criticisms of merchants see John Gregory Bourke, *On the Border with Crook* (New York: C. Scribner Sons, 1891), p. 95; and A. E. Pierce, "Reminiscences of a Pioneer," *Sons of Colorado* 2(September 1907):7.

17. *Daily Miners' Register* (Central City, Colorado), July 29, 1866; *Arizona Weekly Star* (Tucson), June 23, 1877; *Daily Colorado Miner* (Georgetown), Vol., No. 14 (n.d); and the *Helena Weekly Herald* (Montana), May 2, 1867.

18. *Denver Daily,* April 28, 1867.

19. *Laramie Daily Sentinel* (Wyoming), May 13, 1870.

20. *Montana Post* (Virginia City), November 6, 1864.

21. This point was made by the *Helena Weekly Herald,* May 2, 1867.

22. *Montana Post* (Virginia City), July 15, 1865.

23. *Santa Fe Weekly Post,* December 18, 1869.

24. *Daily Miners' Register* (Central City, Colorado), February 15, 1867. Editorial comment about the private manners and morals of residents can be seen in the *Arizona Miner* (Ft. Whipple), March 9, 1864; *Arizona Daily Star* (Tucson), May 23, 1880; *Arizona Citizen* (Tucson), October 3,1874; *Weekly Nugget* (Tombstone, Arizona), October 2, 1879; *Pueblo Chieftain* (Colorado), September 24, 1868; *Laramie Daily Sentinel* (Wyoming), May 5, 1870; *Weekly Independent* (Deer Lodge, Montana), October 12, 1867: *New North-West* (Deer Lodge, Montana), July 9, 1869; *Helena Weekly Herald* (Montana), January 23, 1868; and *Montana Post* (Virginia City), September 10, 1864. See also A. E. Pierce, "Reminiscences of a Pioneer," *Sons of Colorado* 2(November 1907):5; Samuel A. Bristol, "The Newspaper Press of Wyoming," *Hubert Howe Bancroft Scraps*, Western History Collections, University of Colorado Libraries, Boulder. Useful secondary accounts of this aspect of frontier journalism are Barron Beshoar, "The Strife and Struggle of a Newpaper in the Old West," *The American West* 10(September 1973):44; Kenneth Hufford, "P. W. Dooner, Pioneer Editor of Tucson," *Arizona and the West* 10(Spring 1968):25–42; Pat M. Ryan, "Trail-Blazer of Civilization: John P. Clum's Tucson and Tombstone Years," *The Journal of Arizona History* 6(Summer 1965):533–70; Robert J. Goligoske, "Thomas J. Dimsdale: Montana's First Newspaper Editor," (M.A. thesis, Montana State University, 1965), *passim;* Oliver Knight, *"The Owyhee Avalanche:* The Frontier Newspaper as a Catalyst in Social Change," *Pacific Northwest Quarterly* 58(April 1967):74–81.

25. *Boulder County Pioneer* (Colorado), March 31, 1869.

26. *Colorado Miner* (Georgetown), July 16, 1868. See also the *Colorado Weekly Republican* (Denver), February 13, 1862; and the *Weekly Independent* (Deer Lodge, Montanta), February 28, 1868.

27. *Colorado Miner* (Georgetown), February 6, 1868.

28. *Weekly New Mexican* (Santa Fe), March 5, 1864.

29. *Arizona Citizen* (Tucson), August 15, 1874.

30. *Montana Post* (Virginia City), March 21, 1866. Similar statements appear in the *Sweetwater Mines* (South Pass City, Wyoming), May 27, 1868; *Weekly Rocky Mountain Herald* (Denver), June 2, 1860; and *Daily Mining Journal* (Black Hawk, Colorado), January 13, 1864.

31. *Montana Post* (Virginia City), December 3, 1864.

32. *Montana Radiator* (Helena), February 24, 1866.

33. *Boulder County News* (Colorado), October 18, 1872.

34. *Montana Post* (Virginia City), February 25, 1865.

35. *Pueblo Chieftain* (Colorado), August 27, 1868.

36. *Daily Miners' Register* (Central City, Colorado), August 18, 1866.

37. *Weekly Rocky Mountain News* (Denver), October 20, 1859.

38. *Daily Mining Journal* (Black Hawk, Colorado), April 4, 1864.

39. *Santa Fe Weekly Post*, October 21, 1871.

40. *Mining Life* (Silver City, New Mexico), July 26, 1873.

41. *Missoula Pioneer* (Montana), July 6, 1871.

42. *Weekly Rocky Mountain News* (Denver), October 13, 1859. The importance of education is stressed in *The News and Press* (Cimarron, New Mexico), June 24, 1880; *Tri-Weekly Miners' Register* (Central City, Colorado), October 8, 1862; *Helena Daily Herald* (Montana), February 3, 1872; and *Montana Post* (Virginia City), September 17, 1864. See also Paul C. Phillips, ed., *Forty Years on the Frontier as Seen in the Journals and Reminiscences of Granville Stuart, Gold-Miner, Trader, Merchant, Rancher and Politician* (Cleveland: The Arthur H. Clark Company, 1925), II, pp. 30–31; and Margaret Ronan, "Memoirs of a Frontier Woman: Mary C. Ronan," (M.A. thesis, State University of Montana, 1932), pp. 52–53.

43. *Arizona Miner* (Prescott), May 9, 1866.

44. *News and Press* (Cimarron, New Mexico), April 28, 1881.

45. *Laramie Daily Sentinel* (Wyoming), September 27, 1870.

46. *Daily Mining Journal* (Black Hawk, Colorado), February 4, 1865.

47. Thomas J. Dimsdale, *The Vigilantes of Montana: Or Popular Justice in the Rocky Mountains*, with an Introduction by E. De Golyer (Norman: University of Oklahoma Press, 1953), p. 14.

48. *Tri-Weekly Miners' Register* (Central City, Colorado), July 28, 1862. The paper returned to this theme on many occasions. See the issues for April 18, 1863 and April 22, 1863.

49. *Laramie Daily Sentinel* (Wyoming), September 26, 1870.

50. *Weekly Rocky Mountain News* (Denver), February 5, 1863.

51. *Grant County Herald* (Silver City, New Mexico), September 29, 1877. See also the *Cimarron News* (New Mexico), February 7, 1874.

52. *Missoula Pioneer* (Montana), July 6, 1871.

53. *Laramie Daily Sentinel* (Wyoming), November 15, 1870.

54. *Daily New Mexican* (Santa Fe), March 1, 1870.

55. Ibid., December 26, 1871.

56. *Daily Rocky Mountain News* (Denver), April 24, 1869.

57. For the role of editors in fostering the theater in Denver see Dean C.

Nichols, "Pioneer Theaters of Denver, Colorado," (Ph.D. diss. University of Michigan, 1938), pp. 377ff.

58. Mollie E. Dorsey Sanford, "Diary," *The Westerner Denver Posse Brand Book* 10(1954):317.

59. *Arizona Citizen* (Tucson), November 30, 1872.

60. Ibid.

61. *Missoula Pioneer* (Montana), September 21, 1871.

62. *Weekly Colorado Miner* (Georgetown), May 12, 1870.

63. *Weekly Rocky Mountain News* (Denver), June 6, 1860. A more reliable description of the woman population is in the *Daily Missouri Democrat* (St. Louis), December 28, 1859.

Bibliography

NEWSPAPERS

Arizona Citizen(Tucson; Florence). Daily and Weekly.
Arizonan (Tucson). Weekly.
Arizonian (Tubac; Tucson). Weekly and Occasionally.
Arizonian (Tucson). New Series. Weekly.
Arizona Miner (Ft. Whipple; Presott). Daily and Weekly.
Arizona Sentinel (Arizona City; Yuma). Weekly.
Arizona Silver Belt (Globe). Weekly.
Arizona Star (Tucson). Daily and Weekly.
Avant Courier (Bozeman, Montana). Weekly.
Boulder County News (Boulder, Colorado). Weekly.
Boulder County Pioneer (Boulder, Colorado). Weekly.
Canon City Times (Colorado). Weekly.
Caribou Post (Colorado). Weekly.
Cheyenne Leader (Wyoming). Weekly.
Cimarron News (New Mexico). Weekly.
Colorado Leader (Denver). Weekly.
Colorado Miner (Georgetown). Daily and Weekly.
Colorado Republican (Denver). Weekly.
Colorado Transcript (Golden). Weekly.
Colorado Tribune (Denver). Daily and Weekly.
Commonwealth and Republican (Denver). Weekly.
Commonwealth (Denver). Daily and Weekly.
Denver Daily (Colorado). Daily.
Denver Gazette (Colorado). Daily.
Denver Times (Colorado). Daily and Weekly.
Grant County Herald (Silver City, New Mexico). Weekly.
Helena Herald (Montana). Daily and Weekly.
Independent (Deer Lodge and Helena, Montana). Weekly.
Laramie Sentinel (Wyoming). Daily and Weekly.
Madisonian (Virginia City, Montana). Weekly.
Mining Journal (Black Hawk, Colorado). Daily and Weekly.
Mining Life (Silver City, New Mexico). Weekly.

Miners' Register (Central City, Colorado). Daily, Tri-Weekly and Weekly.
Mesilla Times (New Mexico). Weekly.
Missoula and Cedar Creek Pioneer (Missoula, Montana). Weekly.
Missoula Pioneer (Montana). Weekly.
Missoulian (Montana). Weekly.
Missouri Democrat (St. Louis). Daily.
Montana Democrat (Virginia City). Weekly.
Montana News-Letter (Helena). Occasionally.
Montana Pioneer (Missoula). Weekly.
Montana Post (Virginia City and Helena). Daily and Weekly.
Montana Radiator (Helena). Weekly.
Montanian (Helena and Virginia City). Weekly.
Nebraska Republican (Omaha). Weekly.
New Mexican (Santa Fe). Daily and Weekly.
New North-West (Deer Lodge, Montana). Daily and Weekly.
News and Press (Cimarron, New Mexico). Weekly.
New Southwest and Grant County Herald (Silver City, New Mexico). Weekly.
Owyhee Avalanche (Ruby City, Idaho). Weekly.
Pioneer (Missoula). Weekly.
Pueblo Chieftain (Colorado). Weekly.
Register-Call (Central City, Colorado). Weekly.
Republican (Helena, Montana). Tri-Weekly.
Republican Review (Albuquerque, New Mexico). Weekly.
Rio Abajo Press (Albuquerque, New Mexico). Weekly.
Rocky Mountain Gazette (Helena, Montana). Daily and Weekly.
Rocky Mountain Gold Reporter (Mountain City, Colorado). Weekly.
Rocky Mountain Herald (Denver). Daily and Weekly.
Rocky Mountain Herald (Denver). New Series. Weekly.
Rocky Mountain News (Denver). Daily and Weekly.
Santa Fe Gazette (New Mexico). New series. Weekly.
Santa Fe Post (New Mexico). Daily and Weekly.
South Pass News (South Pass City, Wyoming). Weekly.
Sweetwater Mines (South Pass City, Wyoming). Weekly.
The Times (Leavenworth, Kansas). Daily.
The Nugget (Tombstone, Arizona). Daily.
Tombstone Epitaph (Arizona). Daily and Weekly.
The Tribune (Silver City, New Mexico). Weekly.
Union Vedette (Camp Douglas, Utah). Weekly.
Western Mountaineer (Golden City, Colorado). Weekly.

ARCHIVAL COLLECTIONS AND DOCUMENTS

Bachelder, John L. *Reminiscences* (As told to Mrs. George Kitt, 1925). Arizona Historical Society, Tucson.
Bancroft, Hubert Howe. *Hubert Howe Bancroft Scraps.* Western History Collection, University of Colorado Libraries, Boulder.

Banta, Albert Franklin. *Arizona Newspapers: Past and Present*. Department of Library and Archives, Phoenix, Arizona.

Bristol, Samuel A. "The Newspaper Press of Wyoming.' *Hubert Howe Bancroft Scraps*. Western History Collection, University of Colorado Libraries, Boulder.

Brown, R. C. *R. C. Brown Papers*. Arizona Historical Society, Tucson.

Byers, William N. *William N. Byers Papers*. Western History Collection, University of Colorado Libraries, Boulder.

Canfield, Andrew N. *Diary*. Montana Historical Society, Helena.

Carple, R. A. *Reminiscences* (As told to Mrs. George Kitt, 1926). Arizona Historical Society, Tucson.

Chaplin, W. E. "Some of the Early Newspapers of Wyoming." *Wyoming Historcal Society Miscellanies*. Western History Collection, University of Wyoming Library, Laramie.

Clagett, William Horace. *William Horace Clagett Family Papers*. Montana Historical Society, Helena.

Clum, John P. *John P. Clum Papers*. Special Collections, University of Arizona Library, Tucson.

Dailey, John L. *John L. Dailey Papers*. Western History Collection, Denver Public Library.

Dake, Crawley P. *Correspondence*. Special Collections, University of Arizona, Tucson.

Durrield, Milton B. *Miscellanies*. Department of Library and Archives, Phoenix, Arizona.

Fireman, Bert. *What Comprises Treason? Testimony of Proceedings Against Sylvester Mowry*. Department of Library and Archives, Phoenix, Arizona.

Fisk, Andrew J. *Recollections*. Montana Historical Society, Helena.

Fisk, Robert E. *Fisk Family Papers*. Montana Historical Society, Helena.

Fourr, William. *Autobiography*. Arizona Historical Society, Tucson.

Hall, Frank. *Frank Hall Papers*. Western History Collection, Denver Public Library.

Hand, George O. *Diary*. Arizona Historical Society, Tucson.

Hawley, H. G. *Diary*. Documentary Resources Department, State Historical Society of Colorado, Denver.

Hedges, Cornelius. *Cornelius Hedges Family Papers*. Montana Historical Society, Helena.

Herdon, Sallie R. *Dairy*. Montana Historical Society, Helena.

Jacobs, L. M. *L. M. Jacobs Family Papers*. Arizona Historical Society, Tucson.

Maginnis, Martin. *Martin Maginnis Family Papers*. Montana Historical Society, Helena.

Maxwell, James P. *How the First Newspaper Came to Boulder*. Western History Collection, University of Colorado Libraries, Boulder.

Maxwell Land Grant Company Papers. Special Collections Department, University of New Mexico General Library, Albuquerque, New Mexico.

Orahood, Harper M. *Harper M. Orahood Papers*. Western History Collections, Universty of Colorado Libraries, Boulder.

Parsons, George Whitwell. *The Private Journal of George Whitwell Parsons, 1879–1882*. Arizona Historical Society, Tucson.

Plassmann, Martha Edgerton. *Autobiography*. Montana Historical Society, Helena.

Rogers, Isaac. *Diary*. Montana Historical Society, Helena.

Sanders, Wilbur Fisk. *Wilbur Fisk Sanders Family Papers*. Montana Historical Society, Helena.

Skidmore, William H. *William H. Skidmore Family Papers*. Rio Grande Historical Collections, New Mexico State University, Las Cruces, New Mexico.

Slack, E. A. *E. A. Slack Scrapbook*. State of Wyoming Archives, Cheyenne.

Stanton, Frederick J. *Frederick J. Stanton Correspondence*. State of Wyoming Archives, Cheyenne.

Frederick J. Stanton Papers. Western History Collection, Denver Public Library.

Thomas, W. R. *W. R. Thomas Family Papers*. Western History Collection, Denver Public Library.

Tilton, D. W. *D. W. Tilton Papers*. Montana Historical Society, Helena.

Wetter, Henry. *Henry Wetter Papers*. Museum of New Mexico Library, Santa Fe, New Mexico.

Wall, David K. "Interview." *Hubert Howe Bancroft Scraps*. Western History Collection, University of Colorado Libraries, Boulder.

Woodbury, Roger W. "Interview." *Hubert Howe Bancroft Scraps*. Western History Collection, University of Colorado Libraries, Boulder.

Wolff, Joseph. *How the First Newspaper Came to Boulder*. Western History Collection, University of Colorado Libraries, Boulder.

PUBLISHED CONTEMPORARY MATERIALS

Ashley, Susan Riley "Reminiscences of Colorado in the Early 'Sixties." *The Colorado Magazine* 13 (November 1936): 219–30.

Athearn, Robert G., ed. "Life in the Pike's Peak Region: The Letters of Matthew H. Dale." *The Colorado Magazine* 32(April 1955): 81–104.

Baker, Thomas. "Pencil Pictures of Pioneer Pencillers." *Rocky Mountain Magazine* 2(March 1901):540–55.

Barney, Libeus. *Letters of the Pike's Peak Gold Rush: Early Day Letters of Libeus Barney, Reprinted from the Bennington Banner, Vermont, 1859–1860*. San Jose, Calif.: The Talisman Press, 1959.

Beal, W. J. "A Pioneer Woman's Recollection of People and Events Connected with Montana's Early History." *Contributions to the Historical Society of Montana* 8:295–303.

Blake, Henry N. "The First Newspaper of Montana." *Contributions to the Historical Society of Montana* 5:253–64.

Bourke, George Gregory. *On the Border With Crook*. New York: C. Scribner Sons, 1891.

Carroll, John Alexander, ed. *Pioneering in Arizona; the Reminiscences of*

Emerson Oliver Stratton and Edith Stratton Kitt. Tucson: Arizona Pioneers' Historical Society, 1964.

Chaplin, W. E. "Wyoming Scrapbook: Some Wyoming Editors I have Known." *Annals of Wyoming* 18 (January 1946):79–85.

Clum, John P. "It All Happened in Tombstone." *Arizona Historical Review* 2(October 1929):46–72.

[Coutant]. "From Coutant Notes." *Annals of Wyoming* 5(July 1927):36–38.

Crofutt, George A. *Crofutt's Grip-Sack Guide of Colorado; A Complete Encyclopedia of the State.* Vol. 1. Omaha: The Overland Publishing Company, 1881.

Davis, Herman S., ed. *Reminiscences of General William Larimer and of his Son William H. H. Larimer, Two of the Founders of Denver City.* Pittsburgh: Privately Printed, 1918.

De Tocqueville, Alexis. *Democracy in America.* Edited by Richard D. Heffner. New York: The New American Library, 1956.

Dilke, Charles Wentworth (Sir). *Greater Britain: A Record in English-Speaking Countries during 1866 and 1867.* New York: Harper & Brothers, 1869.

Dimsdale, Thomas G. *The Vigilantes of Montana: Or Popular Justice in the Rocky Mountains.* With an Introduction by E. De Golyer. Norman: University of Oklahoma Press, 1953.

Greeley, Horace. *An Overland Journey, from New York to San Francisco, in the Summer of 1859.* New York: C. M. Saxton, Barker and Co., 1860.

Hafen, Le Roy and Hafen, Ann W., eds. *Reports from Colorado: The Wildman Letters, 1859–1865, With Other Related Letters and Newspapers Reports, 1859.* Glendale, Calif.: The Arthur H. Clark Company, 1961.

Hafen, Le Roy R., ed. *Colorado Gold Rush: Contemporary Letters and Reports, 1858–1859.* Glendale, Calif.: The Arthur H. Clark Company, 1941.

Hill, Alice Polk. *Tales of the Colorado Pioneers.* Denver: Pierson & Gardner, 1884.

Homsher, Lola M., ed. *South Pass, 1868: James Chisholm's Journal of the Wyoming Gold Rush.* Lincoln: University of Nebraska Press, 1960.

Howbert, Irving. *Memories of a Lifetime in the Pike's Peak Region.* Glorieta, New Mexico: The Rio Grande Press, Inc., 1970.

Lanford, Nathaniel Pitt. *Viligante Days and Ways: The Pioneers of the Rockies, the Makers and Making of Montana, Idaho, Oregon, Washington and Wyoming.* With an Introduction by Dorothy M. Johnson. Missoula: Montana State University Press, 1957.

Mills, James H. "Reminiscences of an Editor." *Contributions to the Historical Society of Montana* 5:273–88.

Mumey, Nolie, ed. *Alexander Taylor Rankin: His Diary and Letters.* Boulder, Colo.: Johnson Publishing Company, 1966.

———— *Nathan Addison Baker.* Denver: The Old West Publishing Company, 1965.

Morrison, John D., ed. "The Letters of Daniel F. Spain: Gregory's Grubstakes at the Diggings." *The Colorado Magazine* 35(April 1958):81–112.

Morrison, Sidney B. "Letter from Colorado, 1860–1863." *The Colorado Magazine* 16(May 1939):90–96.

Oury, William S. "The Pioneer Press." *Arizona Daily Star*, November 29, 1879.

Phillips, Paul C., ed. *Forty Years on the Frontier as Seen in the Journals and Reminescences of Granville Stuart, Gold-Miner, Trader, Merchant, Rancher and Politician.* 2 vols. Cleveland: The Arthur H. Clark Company, 1925.

Pierce, A. E. "Reminiscences of a Pioneer." *Sons of Colorado* 2(September 1907):3–9.

———— "Reminiscences of a Pioneer." *Sons of Colorado* 2(*October 1907*):3–11.

———— "Reminiscences of a Pioneer." *Sons of Colorado* 2(*November 1907*):3–8.

Plassmann, Martha Edgerton. "Biographical Sketch of Hon. Sidney Edgerton." *Contributions to the Historical Society of Montana* 3:331–40.

Richardson, Albert D. *Beyond the Mississippi: From the Great River to the Great Ocean.* Hartford, Conn.: American Publishing Company, 1873.

Ronan, Peter. "Discovery of Alder Gulch." *Contributions to the Historical Society of Montana* 3:143–52.

"Early Days in Canon City: An Interview with Anson S. Rudd in 1884." *The Colorado Magazine* 7(May 1930):109–13.

Sanford, Mollie E. Dorsey. "Diary." *The Westerners Denver Posse Brand Book* 10(1954):295–329.

Scott, Senator. "Experiences in Colorado in 1859." *The Trail* 11(April 1919): 5–14.

Smith, Dwight L., ed. *John D. Young and the Colorado Gold Rush.* Chicago: R. R. Donnelley & Sons Company, 1969.

Stanton, Irving W. *Sixty Years in Colorado: Reminiscences and Reflections of a Pioneer of 1860.* With an Introduction by Thomas F. Dawson. Denver: Privately Printed, 1922.

Taylor, Bayard. *Colorado: A Summer Trip.* New York: G. P. Putnam and Son, 1867.

Tuttle, Daniel S. *Reminiscences of a Missionary Bishop.* New York: Thomas Whittaker, 1906.

Villard, Henry. *The Past and Present of the Pike's Peak Gold Regions.* Edited by Le Roy R. Hafen. Princeton: Princeton University Press, 1932.

———— *Memoirs of Henry Villard: Journalist and Financier, 1835–1900.* 2 vols. Boston: Haughton, Mifflin and Company, 1904.

Webster, N. H. "Journal of N. H. Webster," *Contributions to the Historical Society of Montana* 3:300–30.

BOOKS

Ashton, Wendell, Jr. *Voice in the West: Biography of a Pioneer Newspaper.* New York: Duell, Sloan & Pearce, 1950.

Athearn, Robert G. *High Country Empire: The High Plains and Rockies.* New York: McGraw-Hill Book Company, Inc., 1960.

———— *The Coloradans.* Albuquerque: University of New Mexico Press, 1976.

Axelrad, Jacob. *Philip Freneau: Champion of Democracy.* Austin and London: University of Texas Press, 1967.

Billington, Ray Allen. *America's Frontier Heritage*. New York: Holt, Rine-hart and Winston, 1966.

Blumberg, Nathan B., and Brier, Warren J., eds. *A Century of Montana Journalism*. Missoula, Montana: Mountain Press Company, 1971.

Boorstin, Daniel J. *The Americans: The National Experience*. Vintage Books. New York: Random House, 1965.

Byers, William N. *Encyclopedia of Biography of Colorado*. 2 vols. Chicago: The Century Publishing and Engraving Company, 1901.

Cleaveland, Norman. *The Morleys–Young Upstarts on the Southwest Frontier*. Albuquerque: Calvin Horn Publishers, Inc., 1971.

Dick, Everett. *The Sod-House Frontier, 1854–1890: A Social History of the Northern Plains from the Creation of Kansas and Nebraska to the Admission of the Dakotas*. New York: D. Appleton-Century Company, 1937.

Dorsett, Lyle W. *The Queen City: A History of Denver*. Boulder, Colo.: Pruett Publishing Company, 1977.

Eaton, Clement. *The Growth of Southern Civilization, 1790–1860*. New York: Harper & Row, 1961.

———— *The Freedom-of-Thought Struggle in the Old South*. Revised edition. New York: Harper & Row, Publishers, Inc., 1964.

Emery, Edwin. *The Press and America: An Interpretative History of the Mass Media*. Third edition, revised. Englewood Cliffs, N.J.: Prentice-Hall, Inc., 1972.

Ferril, Thomas Hornsby and Ferril, Helen, eds. *The Rocky Mountain Herald Reader*. New York: William Morrow & Company, Inc., 1966.

Fritz, Percy Stanley. *Colorado: The Centennial State*. New York: Prentice-Hall, Inc., 1941.

Hafen, Le Roy R., ed. *Colorado and Its People: A Narrative and Topical History of the Centennial State*. 4 vols. New York: Lewis Historical Publishing Co., Inc., 1948.

Hage, George S. *Newspapers on the Minnesota Frontier, 1849–1860*. St. Paul: Minnesota Historical Society, 1967.

Hall, Frank. *History of the State of Colorado . . . .* 4 vols. Chicago: The Blakely Printing Company, 1889.

Hollister, Ovando J. *The Mines of Colorado*. Springfield, Mass.: Samuel Bowles & Company, 1867.

Karolevitz, Robert F. *Newspapering in the Old West: A Pictorial History of Journalism and Printing on the Frontier*. Seattle: Superior Publishing Company, 1965.

Kobre, Sidney. *Development of American Journalism*. Dubuque, Iowa: Wm. C. Brown Company Publishers, 1969.

La Farge, Oliver. *Santa Fe: The Autobiography of a Southwestern Town*. Norman: University of Oklahoma Press, 1959.

Larson, T. A. *History of Wyoming*. Lincoln: University of Nebraska Press, 1965.

Lavender, David. *The Big Divide*. Garden City, N.Y.: Doubleday and Company, Inc., 1949.

———— *The Southwest*. New York: Harper & Row Publishers, 1980.

Leary, Lewis. *That Rascal Freneau: A Study in Literary Failure.* New York: Octagon Books, Inc., 1964.

Lee, James Melvin. *History of American Journalism.* New York: Houghton Mifflin Company, 1917.

Levy, Leonard W. *Jefferson & Civil Liberties: The Darker Side.* Cambridge, Mass.: The Belknap Press of Harvard University Press, 1963.

———— *Legacy of Suppression: Freedom of Speech and Press in Early American History.* Cambridge, Mass.: The Belknap Press of Harvard University Press, 1960.

Lewis, Marvin, ed. *The Mining Frontier: Contemporary Accounts from the American West in the Nineteenth Century.* Norman: University of Oklahoma Press, 1967.

Lutrell, Estelle. *Newspapers and Periodicals of Arizona, 1859–1911.* Tucson: University of Arizona Press, 1950.

Lyon, William H. *The Pioneer Editor in Missouri, 1808–1860.* Columbia: University of Missouri Press, 1965.

McClintock, James H. *Arizona: Prehistoric, Aboriginal, Pioneer, Modern.* 3 vols. Chicago: S. J. Clarke Publishing Company, 1916.

Mott, Frank Luther. *American Journalism, A History: 1690–1960.* Third edition. New York: The Macmillan Company, 1962.

Myers, John Myers. *Print in a Wild Land.* Garden City, N.Y.: Doubleday & Company, Inc., 1967.

Nevins, Allan. *The Evening Post: A Century of Journalism.* New York: Russell & Russell, 1968.

Nichols, Roy Franklin. *The Disruption of American Democracy.* The Free Press. New York: The Macmillan Company, 1948.

Oehlerts, Donald E. *Guide to Colorado Newspapers, 1859–1963.* Denver: Bibliographical Center for Research, Rocky Mountain Region, Inc., 1964.

Paul, Rodman Wilson. *Mining Frontiers of the Far West, 1848–1880.* New York: Holt, Rinehart and Winston, 1963.

———— *California Gold: The Beginning of Mining in the Far West.* Lincoln: University of Nebraska Press, 1964.

Perkin, Robert L. *The First Hundred Years: An Informal History of Denver and the Rocky Mountain News.* Garden City, N.Y.: Doubleday and Company, Inc., 1959.

Sacks, B. *Be It Enacted: The Creation of the Territory of Arizona.* Phoenix: Arizona Historical Foundation, 1964.

Schellie, Don. *The Tucson Citizen: A Century of Arizona Journalism.* Tucson: Tucson Daily Citizen, 1970.

Schlesinger, Arthur H. *Prelude to Independence: The Newspaper War on Britain, 1764–1776.* New York: Alfred A. Knopf, 1958.

Schmitt, Jo Ann. *Fighting Editors: The Story of Editors Who Faced Six-Shooters with Pens and Won.* San Antonio, Texas: The Naylor Company, 1958.

Smiley, Jerome C. *History of Denver.* Denver: The Times-Sun Publishing Company, 1901.

———— *Semi-Centennial History of the State of Colorado.* 2 vols. Chicago: Lewis Publishing Co., 1913.

Smith, Duane A. *Rocky Mountain Mining Camps: The Urban Frontier.* Bloomington: Indiana University Press, 1967.

Sprague, Marshall. *Colorado: A Bicentennial History.* New York: W. W. Norton, 1976.

Stone, Wilbur Fisk. *History of Colorado.* 4 vols. Chicago: S. J. Clark Publishing Co., 1918–19.

Stratton, Porter A. *The Territorial Press of New Mexico, 1834–1912.* Albuquerque: University of New Mexico Press, 1969.

Ubbelohde, Carl, ed. *A Colorado Reader.* Revised edition. Boulder, Colo.: Pruett Press, Inc., 1964.

Ubbelohde, Carl; Benson, Maxine; and Smith, Duane A. *A Colorado History.* Third edition. Boulder, Colo.: Pruett Press, Inc., 1972.

Uchill, Ida Libert. *Pioneers, Peddlers, and Tsadikim.* Denver: Sage Books, 1957.

Wade, Richard C. *The Urban Frontier: The Rise of the Western Cities, 1790–1830.* Cambridge, Mass.: Harvard University Press, 1959.

Walsh, Justin E. *To Print the News and Raise Hell!* Chapel Hill: The University of North Carolina Press, 1968.

Wentz, Roby. *Eleven Western Presses: An Account of How the First Printing Press Came to Each of the Eleven States.* Los Angeles: Privately Printed, 1956.

Wharton, Julius E. *History of the City of Denver from Its Earliest Settlement to the Present Time.* Denver: Byers and Daily, 1866.

Workers of the Writers' Program of the Work Projects Administration in the State of Colorado. *Colorado: A Guide to the Highest State.* New York: Hastings House, 1941.

Wyllys, Rufus Kay. *Arizona: The History of a Frontier State.* Phoenix: Hobson & Herr, 1950.

ARTICLES

Alisky, Marvin. "Arizona's First Newspaper, *The Weekly Arizonian,* 1859." *New Mexico Historical Review* 34(April 1959):134–43.

Bemis, Edwin A. "Journalism in Colorado," in Hafen, Le Roy R., ed. *Colorado and Its People: A Narrative and Topical History of the Centennial State* 2:246–78.

Beshoar, Barron. "The Strife and Struggle of a Newspaper in the Old West." *The American West* 10(September 1973):44–50.

Blodgett, Ralph E. "Colorado Territorial Board of Immigration." *The Colorado Magazine* 46(Summer 1969):245–56.

Burrage, Frank Sumner. "Bill Nye, 1850–1896." *Annals of Wyoming* 11(January 1939):42–49.

Cochran, Alice. "Jack Langrishe and the Theater of the Mining Frontier." *The Colorado Magazine* 7 (Fall 1969):324–37.

Davidson, Levette Jay. "O. J. Goldrick, Pioneer Journalist." *The Colorado Magazine* 8(January 1936):26–37.

De Loney, Burton. "Press on Wheels." *Annals of Wyoming* 14(October 1942):299–306.

Dykstra, Robert R. "Dykstra Rides Again: An Author's Reply to a Critic." *Journal of the West* 10(October 1971):761–66.

Ellison, Rhoda Coleman. "Newspaper Publishing in Frontier Alabama." *Journalism Quarterly* 23(September 1946):289–301.

Gease, Deryl V. "William Byers and the Colorado Agricultural Society." *The Colorado Magazine* 43(Fall 1966):325–38.

Goldrick, O. J. "The First School in Denver." *The Colorado Magazine* 6(March 1929):72–74.

Gurian, Jay. "Sweetwater Journalism and Western Myth." *Annals of Wyoming* 36(April 1964):79–88.

Hafen, Le Roy. "Ghost Towns—Tarryall and Hamilton." *The Colorado Magazine* 10(July 1933):137–42.

Hafen, Le Roy, Fynn, A. J. "Early Education in Colorado." *The Colorado Magazine* 12(January 1935):16–19.

Hall, Martin Hardwick. "The Mesilla Times: A Journal of Confederate Arizona." *Arizona and the West* 5 (Winter 1963): 337–51.

Higgins, Frances. "Sniktau: Pioneer Journalist." *The Colorado Magazine* 5(June 1928):102–8.

Housman, Robert L. "Pioneer Montana's Journalistic 'Ghost' Camp—Virginia City." *The Pacific Northwest Quarterly* 29(January 1938):53–59.

———— "Boy Editors of Frontier Montana." *The Pacific Northwest Quarterly* 27(July 1936):219–26.

———— "The Beginnings of Journalism in Frontier Montana." *Frontier and Midland* 15(Summer 1935):3–10.

———— "The Frontier Journals of Western Montana." *The Pacific Northwest Quarterly* 29(July 1938):269–76.

Hufford, Kenneth. "P. W. Dooner: Pioneer Editor of Tucson." *Arizona and the West* 10(Spring 1968): 25–42.

———— "*The Arizona Gazette*, a Forgotten Voice in Arizona Journalism." *The Journal of Arizona History* 7(Winter 1966):182–87.

Jackson, W. Turrentine. "The Fisk Expeditions to the Montana Gold Fields." *The Pacific Northwest Quarterly* 33(July 1942):265–82.

Kimball, Neil W. "George West." *The Colorado Magazine* 27(July 1950): 198–207.

Knight, Oliver. "*The Owyhee Avalanche:* The Frontier Newspaper as a Catalyst in Social Change." *Pacific Northwest Quarterly* 58(April 1967): 74–81.

Lent, John A. "The Press on Wheels: A History of the *Frontier Index*." *Journal of the West* 10 (October 1971):662–99.

Lyon, William H. "The Corporate Frontier in Arizona." *The Journal of Arizona History* 9(Spring 1968): 1–17.

Marshall, Lawrence W. "Early Denver History as Told By Contemporary

Newspaper Advertisements." *The Colorado Magazine* 8(September 1931): 161–73.

McConnell, Virginia. "A Guage of Popular Taste in Early Colorado." *The Colorado Magazine* 46(Fall 1969):338–50.

McMurtrie, Douglas C. "The History of Early Printing in New Mexico, with Bibliography of Known Issues, 1834–1860." *The New Mexico Historical Review* 4(October 1929):372–410.

———— "The Public Printing of the First Territorial Legislature of Colorado." *The Colorado Magazine* 13(March 1936):72–78.

———— "Pioneer Printing in Wyoming." *Annals of Wyoming* 9(January 1933):729–42.

———— "Eastern Records of Early Wyoming Newspapers." *Annals of Wyoming* 15(July 1943):272–75.

Michelson, Siegfried. "Promotional Activities of the Northern Pacific's Land Department." *Journalism Quarterly* 17(December 1940):324–34.

Norris, Wendell W. "The Transient Frontier Weekly as a Stimulant to Homesteading." *Journalism Quarterly* 30(Winter 1953):44–48.

Nye, Bill. "Wyoming Scrapbook: Bill Nye's Experience." *Annals of Wyoming* 16(January 1944):65–70.

Paladin, Vivian A., ed. "Proper Bostonian, Purposeful Pioneer." *Montana, The Magazine of Western History* 14(Autumn 1974):31–56.

Perrigo, Lynn. "The First Decade of Public Schools at Central City." *The Colorado Magazine* 12(May 1935):86–87.

Poston, Lawrence III, ed. "Poston vs Goodwin: A Document on the Congressional Election of 1865." *Arizona and the West* 3(Winter 1961): 351–54.

Ryan, Pat M. "Trail-Blazer of Civilization: John P. Clum's Tucson and Tombstone Years." *The Journal of Arizona History* 6(Summer 1965):53–70.

Sacks, B. "Arizona's Angry Man: United States Marshal Milton B. Duffield, Part II." *The Journal of Arizona History* 8(Summer 1967):91–119.

Savage, William W. "Newspapers and Local History: A Critique of Robert R. Dykstra's *The Cattle Towns*." *Journal of the West* 10(July 1971):572–77.

Sebben, Lily M. "Life of Nathan A. Baker." *The Colorado Magazine* 12(November 1935):220–23.

Thornton, Vic. "Tucson's Pioneer Newspaper." *Arizona Highways* 20(January 1944): 37–40.

Towne, Jackson E. "Printing in New Mexico Beyond Santa Fe and Taos, 1848–1875." *New Mexico Historical Review* 35(April 1960):109–17.

———— "Some Suggestive Characteristics of Early Western Journalism." *Arizona and the West* 1(Winter 1959):352–57.

Turner, Wallace R. "Frank Hall: Colorado Journalist, Public Servant and Historian." *The Colorado Magazine* 53(Fall 1976):328–51.

Wagner, Henry R. "New Mexico Spanish Press." *New Mexico Historical Review* 12(January 1937):1–40.

Watson, Elmo Scott. "The Indian Wars and the Press, 1866–1867." *Journalism Quarterly* 17(December 1940):301–12.

Willard, James F. "Spreading the News of the Early Discoveries of Gold in Colorado." *The Colorado Magazine* 6(May 1929):98–104.

Working, D. W. "Some Forgotten Pioneer Newspapers." *The Colorado Magazine* 4(May 1927):93–100.

THESES AND DISSERTATIONS

Goligoski, Robert J. "Thomas J. Dimsdale: Montana's First Newspaper Editor." M.A. Thesis, Montana State University, 1965.

Gurian, Jay P. "Two Western Mining Commmunities: A Study of Their Actual Development and Their Mythology." Ph.D. Dissertation, University of Minnesota, 1972.

Housman, Robert L. "Early Montana Territorial Journalism as a Reflection of the American Frontier in the New Northwest." Ph.D. Dissertation, University of Missouri, 1934.

Hufford, Kenneth. "The Establishment of Journalism in Arizona, 1859–1871." M.A. Thesis, University of Arizona, 1966.

Kennedy, Lawrence Michael. "The Colorado Press and the Red Men: Local opinion about Indian Affairs, 1859–1870." M.A. Thesis, University of Denver, 1967.

Perrigo, Lynn. "A Social History of Central City, Colorado, 1859–1900." Ph.D. Dissertation, University of Colorado, 1939.

———— "Life in Central City, Colorado as Revealed by *The Register*, 1862–1872." M.A. Thesis, University of Colorado, 1934.

Nichols, Dean C. "Pioneer Theatres of Denver, Colorado." Ph.D. Dissertation, University of Michigan, 1938.

Ronan, Margaret. "Memoirs of a Frontier Woman: Mary C. Ronan." M.A. Thesis, State University of Montana, 1932.

Shinn, Marie M. "Sidelights on Nineteenth Century Colorado History as Revealed by the Letters of Frank Hall." M.A. Thesis, University of Denver, 1960.

Umans, Joseph. "The Territorial Press of Northern and Central Colorado." M.A. Thesis, University of Colorado, 1928.

Index